WORKBOOK

CHAPEAU!
First-Year French

David A. Dinneen
University of Kansas

Madeleine Kernen
Southwestern Missouri State University

WILEY
John Wiley & Sons

New York   Chichester   Brisbane   Toronto   Singapore

ISBN: 0-471-61639-7

Printed in the United States of America

10 9 8 7 6 5 4 3 2 1

Contents

Sample Exam Form

This form is provided to illustrate the format that we suggest for certain oral exercises for exams included in the instructor's edition.

Dictée   (There will sometimes be a title given, here or orally, to suggest the context of what is to follow)

1. _____

2. _____

3. _____

(We give line numbers for each "chunk" and recommend that instructors use those numbers in the second reading--as in the dictations on cassette for the workbook. Note that the line "chunks" are not necessarily sentences. Also, we do not usually dictate punctuation, although some instructors may do so. We expect students to recognize the end of a sentence by context and do not worry about whether or not they include commas that were in the original text.)

Word and Sound Discrimination   You will hear a series of sentences, one for each numbered list below. <u>Rewrite</u>, for each one, the word or expression you hear.

.   / vu - vous - veut /   _____

.   / nous allons - nous avons /   _____

.   / ils ont - ils sont - ils font /   _____

Logical and appropriate response?   You will hear a series of minidialogues. For each one state whether the response was logical and appropriate: if yes, write *oui* , if no, write *non*.

.   _____   2.   _____   3.   _____

V

Written Work

All written work for this class should be done either on the paper provided or on 8 1/2 X 11 lined paper. Always work in ink (preferably black), unless your instructor directs otherwise, and always leave wide margins and skip lines.

Although we do not expect perfection and certainly not near-native style, we do expect students to be particularly careful in their written work. In the first place, the written language is different from the spoken language and requires more attention to form. In the second place, you have more time, more opportunity to check grammar rules and exact meanings of words when you are writing at home.

We recommend to instructors that written work be corrected as follows:

Students submit the work on the day due, following carefully the instructions about format (skip lines, leave margins, use ink). If any students do not follow those instructions, we believe it is proper--and fair to the entire class--to return those papers uncorrected.

Instructor corrects the papers by underlining errors and placing appropriate abbreviations in the margin. See the abbreviation list on the next page. Papers are then returned, with or without an initial grade.

Students make revisions according to the instructor's notes and comments and resubmit the composition.

Instructor checks the revision, makes any necessary additional corrections, and assigns a grade, if appropriate.

The revision process, of course, may be repeated more than once.

Note that this process can be used not only for compositions but for all written work.

Correction Abbreviations

These common abbreviations, along with any additional ones that your instructor may give you, may be used in the correction of your written work. Errors will be underlined, and the appropriate abbreviation written in the margin.

ac	accent mark missing or incorrect
adj	adjective missing or incorrect
adv	adverb missing or incorrect
agr	agreement not properly indicated
angl	anglicism: use a dictionary to find the right word or expression, or reword your sentence
art	article missing or incorrect
aux	auxiliary verb missing or incorrect
c	contraction required or incorrect
conj	conjunction required
el	elision required
d	delete this word or phrase
dobj	direct object form required
gen	gender of noun or adjective incorrect
id	idiomatic construction: check dictionary
inc	incomplete sentence: rewrite
inf	infinitive form required
impv	imperative form required
intg	interrogative form missing or incorrect
inv	inversion of subject and verb required
indobj	indirect object form required
lex	lexical error: check your dictionary
neg	negative form required or incorrect
om	something has been omitted
pl	plural form required
pro	pronoun required or incorrect
pp	past participle required or incorrect
prep	preposition required or incorrect
psnm	person-number of verb or pronoun incorrect
psp	present participle required or incorrect
rflxv	reflexive form required
relpro	relative pronoun required or incorrect
sing	singular form required
sjn	subjunctive form required
sp	spelling error
t	tense incorrect
ext	text was not followed: reread the exercise instructions
wo	word order incorrect: more than a simple transposition is required
??	can't read and/or this passage does not make sense
x...x	everything between x's is to be rewritten

Reading Assignments

1. Start early, not the day before the assignment is due to be discussed in class.

2. First, scan-read the entire passage without looking up any words or even slowing down to guess at the meanings of words you don't recognize immediately. Try simply to get a general idea of what the passage is about.

    **   At no time in this process should you write translations between the lines.**

3. Read the passage a second time, trying to work out the meanings of words you don't know or of constructions that are unfamiliar by using the total context. Do not use the glossary (if one is provided) or a dictionary.

4. Read the passage a third time, using the glossary or a dictionary as needed.

    **   Do not write the English equivalents between the lines: write them, if at all, on separate paper.** We would prefer that you write out only those words that you realize ought to be part of your productive vocabulary. For example, you should write out and study a word like *arbre*, 'tree' if you don't know it, but should simply retain a word like *frêne*, 'ash tree' as part of your receptive vocabulary (i.e., know it is a type of tree, recognize it in future reading or in a dictation, but do not expect to produce it on your own).

5. Put the assignment aside. Some time later, preferably just before you are to discuss it in class, read it again, rapidly.

    Remember that the purpose of a reading assignment is to give you practice <u>reading</u>. You only improve in reading by reading, and you will be tested at the end of each semester/quarter of French on your reading ability. Do not fool yourself by focusing on exercises that accompany certain reading assignments, without giving full attention to the reading process described above. You may succeed in class that day, but you will not succeed as well on later exams.

Plans de Paris

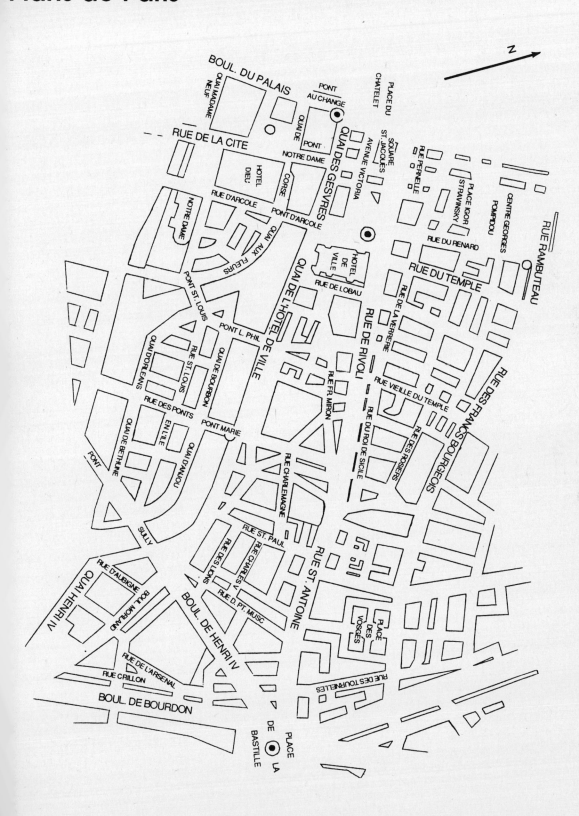

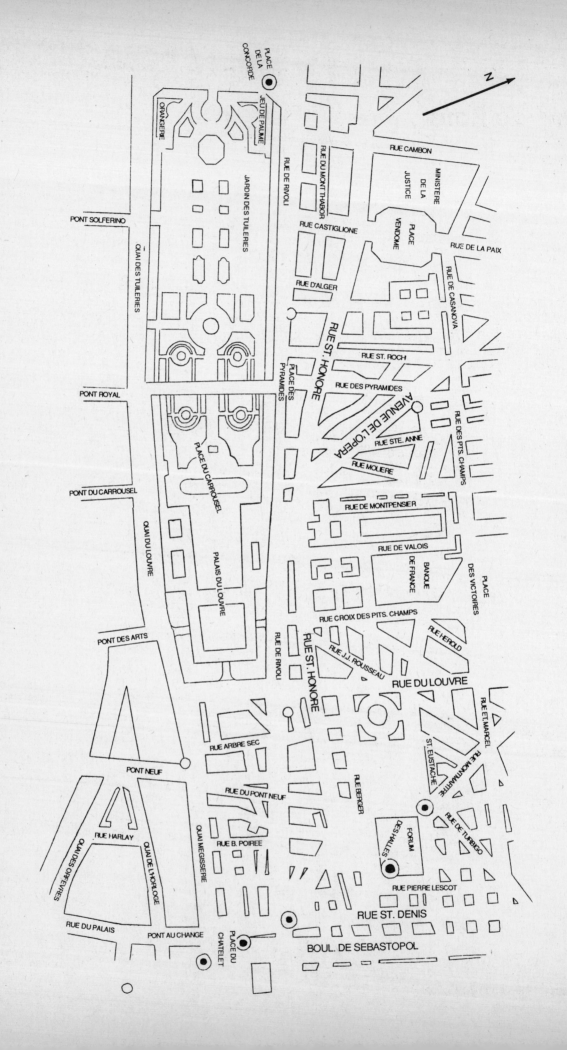

Pour Commencer...

A. *Cassette.* Listen to the robotic and repetitive dialogue. If you have studied the words in the text and attended class, you should be able to understand it easily. Listen at least twice now, and then a few more times later on, not all at once.

B. *Written.* Test yourself. NB: You should be doing this exercise <u>after</u> you have made flashcards and studied the words. After you have tested yourself, check your answers and write in the correct answers for any you missed, <u>in a different-colored ink</u>. Do not erase your mistakes, cross them out: it will be useful for your instructor to know if a number of students missed some of the same words.

a pen _____

a desk _____

the child _____

the dog _____

pants _____

money _____

a head _____

white _____

yellow _____

a bed _____

a green skirt _____

the kitchen _____

a wall _____

a map _____

a young man _____

a student, m . _____

a bra _____

a driver's license _____

a thigh _____

black _____

big _____

a house _____

a good book _____

the hand _____

C. *Cassette.* Listen to Pauline as she describes her family. She doesn't know you are just a beginner and will use quite a few words and constructions you don't know, but that's o.k. All you have to do is try to get the gist of what she says, then answer these questions:

1. Does she have a brother? _____ ... a sister?_____

2. What does her father do? *C'est un* _____.

3. Where does her mother keep her books? _____.

4. Is Pauline bigger than her brothers? _____.

D. *Written.* Complete the blanks for the appropriate words. There should be sufficient context for you to determine what word is missing, but there will be some words used in the sentences that you don't know. You'll have to read each unit (sentence, mini-dialogue, or paragraph) completely in order to figure out what they mean before filling in the blanks.

1. C'est un stylo noir?

    Non, c'est un stylo _____; c'est le stylo du professeur. Il corrige

    les examens avec ce stylo.

2. Marie est étudiante. Elle a un livre et un cahier, mais elle n'a pas de stylo. Ça va, elle a un

    _____.

3. Je suis étudiant. Dans ma chambre il y a un _____ et une

    _____. Mes livres, mes stylos, mes cahiers et mes crayons sont sur la

    _____. Mes vêtements sont sur le _____.

    (Ma mère n'est pas contente.)

4. Madame Renaud est avocate. Elle est très conservatrice. Elle porte toujours un

    _____ gris. Mademoiselle Brune, au contraire, n'est pas conservatrice

    Elle est chanteuse. Elle porte souvent un _____ et une chemise

    d'homme.

Nom _____ **Cours** _____ **Section** _____

E. *Cassette.* Dictée. This will be an easy dictation and it will not be given the way we give dictations in the regular chapters, so enjoy it while you can. Each line will be read twice with a pause each time, for you to write. Listen, write; listen again, make corrections.

1. _____

2. _____

3. _____

4. _____

5. _____

6. _____

7. _____

8. _____

9. _____

10. _____

Nom _____ Cours _____ Section_____

Chapitre Un

Note: Remember that the Workbook is an integral part of this course: it's not just "busy work." In fact, the normal way to prepare for each class is to work quickly through the assigned pages in the textbook, then do the workbook assignment, then review the textbook to see if you can predict what unexpected questions or situations the instructor might introduce at the next class.
It is best to do the workbook exercises for each chapter in order and to have the cassette for that chapter ready to play as you work through the exercises. It is possible to do the oral exercises and written exercises separately, but always be sure to give plenty of time to the oral exercises.

A. *Start the cassette.* First, listen only, glancing rapidly back and forth between the French and the equivalent English expressions.

Répétez tous ensemble.	*Everybody repeat together.*
Répétez, s'il vous plaît.	*Please repeat.*
Comprenez-vous?	*Do you understand?*
Vous comprenez?	*You understand?*
Oui, monsieur.	*Yes, (sir).*
Oui, madame.	*Yes, (Ma'am).*
Oui, mademoiselle.	*Yes, (Miss).*
Posez la même question à votre voisin.	*Ask the same question of the (male) person next to you.*
Tu comprends, Jacques?	*You understand, Jim?*
Non.	*No.*
Posez la même question à votre voisine.	*Ask the same question of the (female) person next to you.*
Tu comprends?	*You understand?*
Oui.	*Yes.*
Qu'est-ce que c'est?	*What is this?*
C'est un livre.	*It's a book.*
Qu'est-ce que c'est?	*What's this?*
Une fleur.	*A flower.*
Qu'est-ce que c'est?	*What are these?*
Ce sont des chiens.	*They're dogs.*

Now listen and repeat, once with the book open if you wish, but at least once with the book closed. Frequent practice of these *expressions utiles* will help prepare you for class.

B. *Written. Qu'est-ce c'est?* Answer the question, "What's this/what are these?" by completing the blank in the first few sentences, then writing the complete answer yourself, following the model (Number 1).

1. It's a book.   1. C'est _____**un livre.**_____
2. It's a table.   2. C'est _____ _____.
3. They're keys.   3. Ce sont _____ _____.
4. It's a pen.   4. C'est _____ _____.
5. It's a wall.   5. _____

6. It's a pencil.   6. _____
7. It's a cat.   7. _____
8. They're walls.   8. _____
9. They're windows.   9. _____
10 It's a door.   10. _____
11. Those are doors.   11. _____
12. It's an elephant.   12. _____

(Now just think of some things that you'd like to know the French words for. Choose <u>concrete</u> objects, not abstract terms. Look each one up in the glossary or a dictionary and complete the next three blanks. If possible, bring the objects--or a drawing--to class.)

13. C'est _____.

14. Ce sont _____.

15. _____

C. *Cassette.* Someone has just incorrectly indentified the object identified between diagonal bars at each line. Following the model, correct him/her. (This is on the cassette: you should listen to it and practice doing dictation; there is no object identification of the last four, just the spoken cues on the cassette.)

Model: /a snake/   Non, ce n'est pas un chat, c'est **un serpent.**

1. /a window/   Non, ce n'est pas une porte, c'est _____.
2. /a pencil/   Non, ce n'est pas une fenêtre, c'est _____.
3. /a set of keys/   Non, ce ne sont pas des professeurs, ce sont _____
                       _____.
4. /a dog/   Non, ce n'est pas un chat, _____.
5. /a (male) student/ Non, ce n'est pas une étudiante, _____.
6. /a bunch of flowers/ Non, ce ne sont pas des éléphants, _____.

(Be sure you use the complete construction, with <u>c'est</u> or <u>ce sont</u>)

7. Non, ce n'est pas une chaise, _____.
8. Non, ce n'est pas un crayon, _____.
9. Non, ce n'est pas un chien, _____.
10. Non, ce ne sont pas des tulipes, _____.

D. *Cassette.* Listen and repeat, looking at both the French and English given below:

1. Comment allez-vous?   *How are you?*
2. Je vais bien, merci.   *I'm fine, thanks.*
3. Et vous?   *And you?*
4. Moi aussi, je vais bien.   *I'm fine too.*
5. Comment vas-tu?   *How are you?*
6. Bien, merci, et toi?   *Fine, thanks, and you?*
7. Comment va Marie?   *How's Mary?*
8. Comment ça va?   *How are you? (familiar)*

E. *Written.* Answer the questions, following the model. If you need to look up the verb form, *aller*, see the Verb Tables, but try first to do the exercise without that help: you've already seen and used all the forms you need.

Model: Comment allez-vous?   **Je vais bien.**

1. Comment vas-tu?   _____
2. Comment va Madelaine?   _____
3. Comment allez-vous? (to group)   _____
4. Comment vont-ils?   _____
5. Comment va Henri?   _____
6. Comment va la famille?   _____

F. *Written.* Answer the questions, following the model. (The forms of *être* are in the Verb Tables.)

Model: Tu es content, toi?   _____ **Oui, je suis content.** _____

1. Est-elle contente?   _____
2. Est-ce que vous êtes contents?   _____
3. Je suis sévère?   _____

(Think! It's the professor asking you a question. How do you address her or him? With what "you" pronoun?)

4. Vous êtes triste?   _____
5. Robert est content?   _____
6. Est-ce qu'ils sont contents?   _____

G. *Cassette.* Repeat as the speaker counts from 0 to 10. Please do not look at the textbook as you do this.

1. 0, 1, 2, ... , 10
2. 0, 2, 4, ... , 10
3. 1, 3, 5, ... , 10
4. 10, 9, 8, ... , 0

H. *Cassette.* Do the addition problems and write the answers in Arabic numerals. The expressions we'll use is "*n* plus *n* font _____? and "*n* plus *n* font _____?"

1. _____ 2. _____ 3. _____ 4. _____ 5. _____ 6. _____

I. *Written.* We'll say someone/something is <u>not</u> X. You complete the statement by providing a contrasting (not necessarily the exact opposite) quality. Keep on the same subject, replacing nouns by *il, elle, ils, elles*.

Model: Jean et Jacques ne sont pas sportifs;...
ils sont studieux.

1. Marie n'est pas studieuse;...

   _____

2. Je ne suis pas bon;...

   _____

3. Tu n'est pas fatigué;...

   _____

4. Marie, Jean, et Robert ne sont pas présents;...

   _____

5. Nous ne sommes pas contents;...

   _____

6. Pierre ne va pas bien;...

   _____

7. Le prof n'est pas sympa;...

   _____

8. Vous n'êtes pas grand;...

   _____

Nom _____ **Cours** _____ **Section** _____

J. *Cassette. Dictée.* There will be three readings. During the first one, listen and try to understand every word. during the second one, write. During the third one, check what you've written, and once again, think about the meaning of the passage or dialogue as a whole. Note: We give line numbers the second time. Those lines do not necessarily correspond to full sentences.

1. _____?
2. _____?
3. _____.
4. _____?
5. _____.
6. _____?
7. _____.
8. _____?
9. _____.
10. _____?

K. *Cassette.* Word and sound discrimination. For each numbered set below, rewrite the word or phrase out of that set that you hear for the corresponding number on the cassette. (Do not write everything you hear, just the word or words from the set on that line.)

1. /un - une/ _____
2. /a - et - est/ _____
3. /la - le/ _____
4. /font - sont - vont/ _____
5. /présent - présente/ _____
6. /la - le/ _____

L. *Written.* On your own. This exercise may be collected separately. Using only the vocabulary and expressions that you remeber (do not look any up), write out a simple conversation between you and a friend you meet outside of class. Start with a greeting, ask how he/she is, ask one or two other simple questions, close with a farewell. Be sure to use *tu* in addressing your friend.

YOU: _____

YOUR FRIEND: _____

YOU: _____

YOUR FRIEND: _____

YOU: _____

YOUR FRIEND: _____

YOU: _____

YOUR FRIEND: _____

YOU: _____

YOUR FRIEND: _____

YOU: _____

YOUR FRIEND: _____

Chapitre Deux

A. *Cassette.* Listen and look back and forth between the French and English equivalents (two readings on tape; you may replay it if you wish).

Répondez à la question.	*Answer the question.*
Dites la même chose à votre voisin.	*Say the same thing to the (male) person sitting next to you.*
Dites la même chose à votre voisine.	*Say the same thing to the (female) person sitting next to you.*
Comment dit-on "happy" en français?	*How do you say "happy" in French?*
On dit "heureux".	*They say "heureux".*
Vous avez compris?	*Did you understand?*
Tu as compris?	*Did you understand?*

B. *Cassette.* Now listen and repeat without looking at the text. (The tapescript will have *expressions utiles* from Chapters 1 and 2, not in the order presented, with some minor variations.)

C. *Cassette.* Read quickly the following English version of the short dialogue in your textbook. Then listen to the recorded version a number of times, without looking at either text.

Teacher:	Hello, Phillipe.
Student:	Hello, ma'am.
Teacher:	What's that, Phillipe?
Student:	It's an elephant.
Teacher:	Oh. What's its name?
Student:	His name is Toto.
Teacher:	You're tired, aren't you? (You must be tired.)
Student:	No, Toto is small.

D. *Cassette.* Listen and repeat, looking at the Arabic numerals. You will be given time to repeat each *set* after it has been read, not each numeral.

Set a.   1, 3, 5, 7, 9
Set b.   2, 4, 6, 8, 10
Set c.   11, 13, 15, 17, 19
Set d.   12, 14, 16, 18. 20
Set e.   21, 23, 25, 27, 29
Set f.   22, 24, 26, 28, 30
Set g.   17, 18, 19, 20, 21
Set h.   20, 22, 21, 29, 23

E. *Cassette.* Listen to the question and response. Fill in the blank with the age given, using Arabic numerals.

1. J'ai _____ ans.

2. J'ai _____ ans.

3. J'ai _____ ans.

4. J'ai _____ ans.

5. Jean-Pierre? Il a _____ ans.

6. Moi? J'ai _____ ans.

7. Oh! oui, il a _____ ans.

F. *Written.* Complete the following sentences, <u>writing out</u> (in French) the age of the person, as given in parentheses, and finally (in sentences 6 - 10) writing out the entire sentence, supplying your own subject (a name, your real brother, . . . see following list for ideas).

(23) Mon frère a _____ ans.   (my brother)

(19) Ma sœur a _____ ans.   (my sister)

(20) Robert a _____ ans.

(21) Jacqueline a _____ ans.

(22) Jean est plus âgé que Robert; il a _____   _____ ans.

Model. (<u>18</u>)   **Mon ami Jean a dix-huit ans.**

(___) _____.

(___) _____.

(___) _____.

(___) _____.

(___) _____.

You may use: mon ami C***   mon amie F***   ma mère
                mon cousin   mon frère   ma sœur
                ma cousine   mon oncle

(Don't look these words up--just guess at their meaning.)

G. *Cassette.* Listen to the following commands, looking back and forth between the French and English equivalents.

Regardez-moi.	*Look at me.*
Donne-moi ce stylo.	*Give me a pen.*
Rendez-moi vos copies.	*Turn in your papers to me.*
Jean, lève-toi.	*John, get up.*
Mlle Legrand, levez-vous.	*Miss Legrand, get up.*
Allez à la porte.	*Go to the door.*
Fermez la porte.	*Open the door.*
Ouvrez la porte.	*Close the door.*
Retournez à votre place.	*Go back to your seat.*
Montez dans le taxi.	*Get in the taxicab.*
Allez à la gare.	*Go to the (railroad) station.*
Allez au guichet deux.	*Go to window 2.*
Achetez un billet.	*Buy a ticket.*
Passez à la caisse.	*Go to the cashier's window.*
Allez au quai deux.	*Go to platform two.*
Compstez votre billet.	*Cancel your ticket. (Put it in a machine that eats a chunk out of it.)*
Marie, donne-moi une bise.	*Give me a little kiss, Mary.*

H. *Cassette.* You will now hear a series of commands, followed by (we hope) appropriate sound effects as the person complies with the request/command. Listen and pay attention. This is not just for amusement, though we're sure it's very entertaining: thses expressions will come up later in class.

I. *Written.* Forms of the definite article (See *Reference Grammar,* 2.2.2 and 21.). · Replace the indefinite article by a definite article (instead of saying 'a book' or 'pens,' we'll say 'the book' or 'the pens'). Rewrite the entire phrase, not just the article.

un stylo _____

une chaise _____

des stylos _____

des chaises _____

un grand livre _____

une belle pomme _____

un ami _____

une amie _____

des amis _____

un homme _____

un petit homme _____

des exercises _____

J.   *Written.* Complete the blanks in the following sentences by using the appropriate word from the "pool" we provide <u>and</u> filling in the proper form of the verb given in parentheses. Be sure to make any contractions that are required. (*Reference Grammar*, 21.)

/ les étudiants - le médecin - le jardin - le mur - l'université - le professeur - l'exercice - le restaurant /

1.   (arriver à) Les enfants _____**arrivent au jardin**_____ avec leurs jouets.

2.   (parler à) Le professeur _____.

3.   (parler à) Quand vous êtes à l'hopital, vous _____.

4.   (parler de) Les étudiants _____ quand il n'est pas dans la salle de classe.

5.   (arriver à) Les étudiants _____ à 8h du matin.

6.   (arriver à) A 6h du soir, nous _____ pour le dîner.

K.   *Written.* Write out the question that would have elicited the answer given. You may use *est-ce que*, inversion, or simply normal word order with a question mark, but don't use just one formula for all sentences. Note that these are all responses to "yes/no" questions, and all involve verbs that follow the same pattern as *regarder*. (For all third-person forms, we give you a subject noun to use, as in the model.)

Model: **Est-ce que Robert regarde cette carte?**
       -- Oui, il regarde cette carte.   (Robert)

1.   _____?

       -- Non, je ne regarde pas cette carte.

2.   _____?

       -- Non, elles ne parlent pas lentement.   (les Françaises)

3.   _____?

       -- Oui, nous regardons le film.

4.   _____?

       -- Oui, monsieur, vous posez beaucoup de questions.

5.   _____?

       -- Non, il ne retourne pas à sa place.   (Phillipe)

6.   _____?

       -- Oui, je ferme la porte.

7.   _____?

       -- Oui, elle entre dans la salle.   (Mademoiselle Caillou)

8.   _____?

       -- Non, il n'explique pas la leçon.   (le professeur)

L. *Written.* Make the following sentences negative, using the simple negative construction. This will seem boring (it is!), but please write out each sentence carefully, thinking what it means: it is important to get the order of negative words straight right now.

Model: Je suis content.
Je ne suis pas content.

1. Nous parlons francais.

   _____

2. Alors, vous êtes content?

   _____

3. Le prof ferme la porte.

   _____

4. Ils regardent le portrait.

   _____

5. Les étudiants entrent dans la salle.

   _____

6. Tu retournes à ta place.

   _____

7. Vous regardez votre livre.

   _____

8. Nous sommes heureux.

   _____

M. *Written.* Make up four simple "yes/no" questions and write the answers, all in the negative--as in the model. Do not use the verb *avoir.*

Model: Etes-vous contente?
Non, je ne suis pas contente.

1. _____?

   Non,_____.

2. _____?

   _____.

3. _____?

   _____.

4. _____?

   _____.

N. *Cassette.* Do the simple calculations requested of you on the cassette. The expressions we'll use are:

for addition: "*n* et n font *n.*" (e.g. Deux et deux font quatre.) OR ("*n* plus *n* font *n.*")
for subtraction: "*n* moins *n* font *n.*" (e.g. Quatre moins deux font deux.)
for multiplication: "*n* fois *n* font *n.*" (e.g. Deux fois deux font quatre.)

Sentences 1 - 5 are dictated completely. Fill in the blanks with the numerals, written in French. Sentences 6 - 10 are "problems"--give the answer only, in Arabic numerals.

1.   __Deux__ plus __quatre__ font _____ .
2.   _____ plus __dix-sept__ font _____ .
3.   __Vingt-cinq__ moins _____ font _____ .
4.   _____ fois __quatre__ font _____ .
5.   __Trente__ moins _____ font _____ .
6.   _____
7.   _____
8.   _____
9.   _____
10. _____

(The only reason we have not included any exercises in division, is that one of your authors hates arithmetic, particularly division--long or short. If you really want to do it in French, the expression is: "*n* divisé par *n* font *n.*" One can also use that kind of expression for multiplication: "*n* multiplié par *n* font *n.*")

O. *Cassette. Dictée.* The dictation will be read three times: once rapidly (listen, do not write), once with pauses (write during the pauses), once again rapidly (make corrections).

"Nous ne voulons pas être comme Claudine."

1.   _____ .
2.   _____ ,
3.   _____ .
4.   _____
5.   _____ .
6.   _____ .
7.   _____ ,
8.   _____ .
9.   _____ !
10. _____ , _____ , _____ !

Nom _____ Cours _____ Section_____

P. *Cassette.* Word and sound discrimination. You will hear a series of five sentences. Each one will contain one of the words or short phrases listed with the corresponding number below. Rewrite the word of phrase you hear, in the blank provided.

1. / est - et - êtes / _____
2. / ville - vie - vite / _____
3. / grand - grande - gant / _____
4. /mauvais - mauvaise / _____
5. /ont - sont - vont / _____

Q. *Written.* Composition. Imagine you have arrived in class early. Write the dialogue that takes place as your instuctor greets you, asks some questions, tells you to get up, to go to the board, or to open/close the door. If you wish, add another person to the dialogue at the end. Before you do this exercise, quickly scan the textbook and/or the workbook to remind yourself of what you are now able to talk about in French--but then DO NOT use the book again until you have finished.

PROF: _____
YOU: _____
PROF: _____
YOU: _____
PROF: _____
YOU: _____
PROF: _____
YOU: _____
    : _____
    : _____
    : _____
    : _____
    : _____
    : _____

Chapitre Trois

A. *Cassette.* Listen only, looking back and forth between the English and French equivalents.

Pardon, monsieur, que veut dire "lentement"?	*Excuse me, sir, what does "lentement" mean?*
Pardon, madame, que veut dire "paresseux"?	*Excuse me, ma'am what does "paresseux" mean?*
Parlez plus fort, s'il vous plaît.	*Please speak louder.*
Parlez plus lentement, s'il vous plaît.	*Talk more slowly, please.*
Allez au tableau noir.	*Go to the blackboard.*
Retournez à votre place.	*Go back to your seat.*
Ouvrez votre livre à la page cinq.	*Open your book(s) to page five.*
Tournez à la page vingt-trois.	*Turn to page twenty-three.*
Passez-moi vos copies, s'il vous plaît.	*Please pass in your papers.*
Posez-moi une question.	*Ask me a question.*
Posez une question à votre voisine.	*Ask a question of the (female) person sitting next to you.*
Fifi, comment vas-tu aujourd'hui?	*How are you today, Fifi?*

B. *Cassette.* Books closed, please. Repeat.
(The recording will contain some of the above sentences, but not in the same order, and with some variations, including some expressions from Chapters 1 and 2.)

C. *Cassette.* Read quickly the following English version of the dialogues in your textbook, then listen once to the recorded version while looking at the French text. After that, listen to the recording a number of times, without looking at either text. Do not try to work out a "translation" by comparing the two texts: the English is provided only to be sure you understand what the dialogues are about, not to have you work on analyzing the grammar of the sentences.

First dialogue:

Narrator: A client enters a men's clothing shop. A saleslady approaches.

Saleslady: Good afternoon, madam. May I help you?

Client: Hello. I'd like to find something for my fiancé's birthday, and it's tomorrow!

Saleslady: I understand. Let's see . . . . Here we have some shirts, and over there you have trousers and suits in wool, in linen, in silk . . . .

Client: Would you have something a bit simpler, for example, some scarves, hats or ties?

Saleslady: Wait here a minute. I'll go look for some beautiful leather ties that just arrived.

Narrator: The client waits for several minutes. Finally, the saleslady reappears.

Saleslady: Here they are. See, I have ties of all colors, brown, blue, grey, red, violet, and they only cost 150 francs.

Client: Excellent idea. Give me a grey tie and green one.

Saleslady: Shall I gift-wrap them?

Client: Yes, please.

Narrator: The client pays and leaves the shop, pleased with her purchase.

Second dialogue:

Pierre: I'm looking at an animal. What is it?

Marie: Is it small?

Pierre: No, it's not small.

Paul: Is it in this room?

Pierre: No, it's in this photograph.

Josée: Is it a lazy animal?

Pierre: No, it's very active.

Paul: Is it nice and pleasant?

Pierre: Yes.

Marie: Is it a cat?

Pierre: No, it's a dog. Cats aren't nice.

D. *Written.* Count nouns. Answer the "yes/no" question, following the model and the indication in parentheses.

Model: Avez-vous des frères? (3)

Oui, j'ai trois frères.

1. Avez-vous des sœurs? (1)

   _____

2. Tu as des frères? (negative response)

   Non,_____

3. Les étudiants ont des stylos? (affirmative)

   Oui,_____

4. Est-ce que le prof a un stylo rouge? (negative)

   _____

5. A-t-il une voiture? (negative)

   _____

6. Mais, il a un vélo, n'est-ce pas? (affirmative)

   _____

7. Tu as des parents ici? (affirmative) (*parents:* 'relatives')

   _____

8. Ont-elles des cahiers? (negative)

   _____

E. *Cassette.*

1. Listen and repeat rapidly. On the first run-through, look at the verb forms here. On subsequent playings, do not look: just listen and repeat. (It is very important that you listen to the verb exercises, in particular, a number of times.)

    je fais, tu fais, il fait   (All three verb forms pronounced the same)
    nous faisons   (Pay attention to the *fai-* part: the sound is different from the way the same letters are pronounced in the first three.)

    vous faites
    ils font

2. Following the model on the tape, give the form (in a full, short sentence) that is required.

F. *Written.* Using the verb *faire*, ask the question that would elicit the answer given.

Model: **Tu fais ton lit tous les jours?**
    -- Oui, je fais mon lit tous les jours.

1. _____?
    -- Oui, mademoiselle, je fais mes devoirs tous les jours.

2. _____?
    -- Non, il ne fait pas de ski.

3. _____?
    -- Oui, nous faisons du camping.

4. _____?
    -- Non, elle ne fait pas son lit tous les matins. *(every morning)*

5. _____?
    -- Oui, ça fait cinq. (Be careful: use a plural verb form.)

6. _____?
    -- Non, vous ne faites pas les devoirs.

G. *Written.* Non-count nouns (mass nouns). Fill in the blank with the proper form of the partitive article.

Model: Il a ___**du**___ courage.

1. Elle a _____ esprit.

2. Nous avons _____ pain.

3. Ils n'ont pas _____ pain.

4. Donnez-moi _____ eau, s'il vous plaît.

5. A-t-il _____ courage? Non, il n'a pas _____ courage.

6. Elle porte toujours _____ parfum.

7. Les riches ont _____ argent; les pauvres n'ont pas _____ argent.

8. Ils vont acheter _____ viande.

9. Elle a _____ élégance: elle commande _____ champagne.

10. Nous commandons _____ bière.

H. *Cassette.* Look at the drawing as you listen to the listing of the objects included in it. (Note that the objects are numbered.) Now answer the questions on the tape. Please DO NOT write out the questions: the simplest way to do this exercise is to take one question at a time, stop the cassette while you answer, start again. Get used to this exercise, because your oral exams may include exercises like it.

1. _____

2. _____

3. _____

4. _____

5. _____

Written. Answer the following questions. You need not be truthful on personal questions, but the answers should be appropriate.

1. Combien de frères avez-vous?

   _____

2. Combien d'amis avez-vous?

   _____

3. Combien d'étudiants y a-t-il dans la classe de français?

   _____

4. Combien de questions est-ce que le professeur pose?

   _____

5. Combien de livres y a-t-il dans la bibliothèque?

   _____

6. Combien d'argent y a-t-il dans votre poche/votre portefeuille?

   _____

Cassette. Dictation of clock-time expressions. Write, in Arabic numerals (following the model), the times that you hear.

Model: Il est six heures et demie.
   ___6h30___

_____   2. _____   3. _____   4. _____

_____   6. _____   7. _____   8. _____

K. *Written.* Write out, completely *(en toutes lettres)* the times given. Add *du matin, de l'après-midi, du soir,* as appropriate.

Model: 8 h 30 --> **Il est huit heures et demie du matin.**

1. 7 h 30 --> _____
2. 14 h 30 --> _____
3. 0 h 10 --> _____
4. 12 h --> _____
5. 15 h 20 --> _____
6. 20 h 30 --> _____
7. 8 h 45 --> _____
8. 10 h 50 --> _____
9. 24 h --> _____
10. 11 h 45 --> _____

L. *Cassette. Word and sound discrimination.* Write the word(s) you hear, in the space provided.

1. / deux heures - dix heures - des heures / _____
2. / moins deux - moins dix - moins douze / _____
3. / du - des - de / _____
4. / ils vont - ils font - ils sont / _____

M. *Cassette. Dictée.*   Discussion entre une mère et sa fille.

1. _____?
2. _____.
3. _____.
4. _____.
5. _____.
6. _____?
7. _____.
8. _____.
9. _____.
10. _____.
11. _____.
12. _____.
13. _____.
14. _____.

N. *Written.   Composition.* Write ten short sentences, each one beginning with a clock time expression followed by an appropriate activity or situation that might occur at that time. Use: *"À X heures, ..."* ('At X o'clock, ...).

Model: **À six heures du matin, je fais mon lit.**

1. _____
2. _____
3. _____
4. _____
5. _____
6. _____
7. _____
8. _____
9. _____
10. _____

Chapitre Quatre

A. *Cassette.* Listen first, then listen and repeat, as explained on the tape.
(The following is a loose translation of the dialogue. Look at it before and/or during your first listening. Do not copy translations into the textbook. Do not look at the following "translation" while repeating.)

Tourist: Hello. I'd like to go to the Rodin museum.

Clerk: Good. Wait here a minute, I'll call a taxi for you.

Tourist: Oh, no thanks. Taxis are too expensive. Besides, it's a beautiful day. I'd rather walk. Could you tell me how to get there on foot?

Clerk: Sure. That's going to be quite a hike.

Tourist: How long?

Clerk: Oh, about a half-hour maybe. Our hotel is on the *Boulevard Saint-Germain.* Turn right as you leave the hotel and go to the *Rue du Bac.* There, turn left and go to the *Rue de Varenne,* where you have to turn right. Keep going in the direction of the *Hôtel des Invalides.* The Rodin museum will be on your left.

Tourist: Thanks very much. And how can I get back by metro?

Clerk: That's a bit more complicated: the metro station is *Varenne.* You take the subway in the direction of *Porte d'Orléans.* At the *Duroc* station, you'll have to transfer: get out and take the subway in the direction of *Gare d'Austerlitz.* You can get out at the *Mabillon* station and you'll be very near the hotel.

Tourist: You weren't kidding: that is pretty complicated.

Clerk: I have a suggestion: go both ways on foot.

Tourist: Thank you. How would you like to visit the museum with me?

Clerk: Great idea. Let me just close the office up and I'll be right with you.

O.K. So no hotel clerk in Paris would close up and go to the museum with a tourist ... There are no live elephants that you can carry around with you either!)

B. *Cassette.* What follows is a quick review of a number of *expressions utiles* introduced in the first three chapters. Listen and simply determine if each one is sufficiently familiar to you: that is, whether or not you understand it. If not, put a check mark next to it and look it up (the chapter and line numbers are given); if you <u>do</u> understand it, just repeat the expression (do not go back and check for the exact meaning).

- Chapter 1, 2
- Chapter 1, 4
- Chapter 2, 1
- Chapter 2, 5
- Chapter 3, 1
- Chapter 3, 3
- Chapter 3, 4
- Chapter 3, 6

C. *Cassette.* Dictation and practice with possessive adjectives. First, write in the question that you hear, as directed on the tape and following the model. Then listen again and respond with the appropriate expression: *le voici, la voici,* or *les voici.* (The correct response is given in the second reading, after a pause.) By the way, there are some words in this exercise that you may not have seen before, but they are all useful, high-frequency items and we've listed them in alphabetical order in the Glossary which follows the exercise.

FIRST READING

Model: You hear: Où est mon livre?

In the pause following that, write: **Où est mon livre?**

1. _____?
2. _____?
3. _____?
4. _____?
5. _____?
6. _____?
7. _____?
8. _____?

SECOND READING

Model: You hear: Où est mon livre?

In the pause following that, you say: **Le voici.**

Glossary:

cheval, *m.*	*horse*	robe, *f.*	*dress*
couteau, *m.*	*knife*	sac, *m.*	*pocketbook*
hôtel, *m.*	*hotel*	soeur, *f.*	*sister*
journal, -aux, *m.*	*newspaper*		

D. *Written.* Write a complete NEGATIVE answer to each question, using the word in parentheses to contradict the questioner, either as to the owner of the item mentioned (we'll provide the appropriate possessive, as in model *a.*), or as to the identification of the item mentioned (see model *b.*).

Models: a. -- Je regarde mon nez, n'est-ce pas? (mon)
            Non, vous regardez mon nez!

(That's not a typo: the questioner says "I'm looking at my nose, right?"; the answerer says "No, you're looking at <u>my</u> nose" -- same word each time, different referent.)

            b. -- Je parle à ton chat, n'est-ce pas? (chien)
            Non, tu parles à mon chien.

(We changed not only the item mentioned, but also the possessive adjective: of course, it still refers to the same owner--the person originally addressed.)

1. C'est mon sac, n'est-ce pas?   (mon)

   _____

2. C'est votre prof?   (ami)

   _____

3. Il parle à sa mère?   (père)

   _____

4. Ce sont vos étudiants?   (enfants)

   _____

5. Tu cherches ton livre?   (devoirs)

   _____

6. Vous entrez dans votre maison?   (appartement)

   _____

7. Ils ferment leur porte, n'est-ce pas?   (fenêtres)

   _____

8. Vous allez dans votre cuisine?   (chambre)

   _____

Written. Fill in the blanks with the appropriate form of the verb *prendre*, or *apprendre*, or *comprendre*. In this particular exercise, it's permissible to use any of the verbs more than once. In some sentences, more than one of the verbs will fit the context.
Note: The verb *prendre* does not mean "take" in the sense of "take a course". (We use *suivre* for that.)

Je _____ un bain.

Nous _____ bien le français.

Tu vas _____ le chinois l'année prochaine?

_____-vous?

Marie et Jean _____ un taxi pour aller à l'aéroport.

On _____ beaucoup dans un cours de linguistique.

Cassette. Verb drill for *prendre, comprendre, apprendre.* Repeat the first short sentence given each time, then give the appropriate follow-up according to the cue, as in the model.

Model: You hear: Je prends le train.   (there's a pause)
          You say: **Je prends le train.**
          Then you hear: Nous.   (pause)
          You say: **Nous prenons le train.**

Note: We'll give three separate cues after each verb phrase. After a pause, during which you should respond, we'll give the correct response. Listen to it carefully and match it with yours but do not repeat it. (There will not be time to do so.)

For third-person forms, instead of a pronoun cue, we'll usually give a noun (*Jacques, Mon ami, Les étudiants, Marie et Françoise*, etc.) to make it clear whether the subject is singular or plural. Always repeat the cue (or the equivalent pronouns) with the verb form, not just the verb form alone.

(These are the cues: in later lessons, we will not give them in written form.)

1. Je prends le train.
2. Tu comprends?
3. Il apprend le français.
4. Elles prennent le métro.
5. Nous comprenons la question.
6. Vous prenez un verre?

G. *Written.* Your very forgetful roommate is moving out (*Dieu merci!*). There were some things that she was not sure about: were they hers or not? So she put them in a big box, waited for you, and is now asking your help/opinion. Complete the responses, using an appropriate possessive adjective. Careful: note that your roommate doesn't always suggest that an item is *hers*.

Model: C'est ma tasse?
-- Oui, **c'est ta tasse.**

1. Ce sont mes photos?

   -- Oui,_____.

2. a. Est-ce mon éléphant?

   -- Non,_____.

   b. C'est peut-être l'éléphant de Marie et de Jeanne?

   -- Oui,_____.

3. a. C'est mon cahier, n'est-ce pas?

   -- Non,_____.

   b. Est-ce le cahier de ton frère?

   -- Oui,_____.

4. Voici mes lunettes de soleil, n'est-ce pas?

   -- Oui,_____.

5. Ce sont tes chaussettes sales?

   -- Non!_____.

Now add two of your own.

6. _____?

   -- _____.

7. _____?

   -- _____.

H. *Written.* Is your room a mess? Look around you (literally or in your imagination) and list items in your room--as you did in an earlier chapter, but this time you're going to locate the items and tell us whose they are, following the model. Try to stay within your vocabulary, but you may use a dictionary if you wish and you certainly are not restricted to mundane items like *livre, stylo.* You may assume you are speaking to a friend on the phone and thus say something like *"Et ta cassette est sur la table."*

Model: **Mon livre est sur le lit.**
Mes devoirs sont dans la corbeille.
La photo de Nanette est sur la table.

(Attention: Remember there is no apostrophe *s* in French.)

1. _____
2. _____
3. _____
4. _____
5. _____
6. _____
7. _____
8. _____

(We hope you used at least five different prepositions. If not, your instructor may be disappointed.)

I. *Written.* Following the model and using the information given you, write out what each person described is. (Some words you'll need are: *avocat, boulanger, athlète, directrice, musicien, médecin.*) In the first five, follow model a.; in the second five, model b. Remember, both forms (*C'est un : il est*) mean essentially the same thing: we want you to become familiar with both because both are used frequently.
Model a: Voici Nanette. Son père et sa mère sont canadiens.
-- Elle est canadienne.

1. Voici Paul. Il apprend le français à cette université.

_____.

2. Voici mes amis. Ils sont religieux. Ils vont à la messe tous les dimanches.

_____.

3. Voici mon père, Il travaille devant les juges.

_____.

4. Voici ma tante. Elle est allée à l'École de Médecine. Elle soigne les malades.

_____.

Model b: Voici Monsieur Dubois. Il est devant la classe. Ce n'est pas un étudiant.
- **C'est un professeur.**

5. Voici Nicole. Elle est née en France. Ses parents sont français.

   _____.

6. Voici Monsieur Bonpain. Il travaille à la boulangerie.

   _____.

7. Voici Claudine Collet. Elle est chef d'une grande compagnie industrielle.

   _____.

8. Voici Philippe LeFort. Il joue au football. Il court vite. Il est costaud.

   _____.

J. *Written.* Complete the following blanks with *il/elle est, c'est, ils/elles sont,* or *ce sont,* as required by the context. At the same time, prepare to answer similar questions in class, or at an exam.

1. Votre père, il est avocat? Non, _____ un médecin.

2. Vos sœurs, sont-elles journalistes? Oui, _____ des journalistes.

3. Et votre mère? _____ professeur.

4. Votre père est sénégalais? Non, _____ algérien.

5. Et votre mère? _____ une Française.

6. Votre mère est catholique? Oui, _____ catholique.

7. Et votre père? Non, _____ luthérien.

K. *Cassette.* You're going to hear a number of different statements, each introducing a telephone number. We'll give you a hint as to the content of the statement, but don't worry if you don't understand each one. All you are <u>required</u> to do is write out the telephone number, in Arabic numerals.

   Model: You hear: - Votre numéro de téléphone, s'il vous plaît.
                            - C'est le 44-62-07-89
              You write: **44-62-07-89**

1. (Phil gets the aswering machine at François' house.)   _____

2. (Radio announces a time and temp service.)   _____

3. (She gives him her telephone number.)   _____

4. (MacDonald's in Paris takes phone orders.)   _____

5. (Operator gives you a number you requested.)   _____

6. (You get an emergency number.)   _____

L. *Written.* Some number-writing practice. Please be sure to do this without looking at the number list in the text, then check it against the key. You're just trying to find out if you remember the basic orthographic conventions, and--as we say--it's not as important as learning to work with numbers orally.

Model: 1 833   **mille huit cent trente-trois**

1. 900 _____
2. 86 _____
3. 264 _____
4. 3 655 _____
5. 91 _____
6. 10 600 _____
7. 321 _____
8. 76 _____
9. 1 765 _____
10. 189,95 _____

M. *Cassette.* Word and sound discrimination. Write out the word(s) you hear in the space provided.

1. / sur - sous - son / _____
2. / il comprend - ils comprennent - nous comprenons / _____
3. / sa - ses - son / _____
4. / vous - votre - vos / _____

N. *Cassette. Dictée.* Follow the instructions given on the cassette (usual format).

"Un ami indiscret"

_____
_____
_____
_____
_____
_____
_____

9. _____

10. _____

11. _____

12. _____

O. *Written.*

(1) Using the "historical present," tell us what happened to you on five significant dates in your life. Write no more than two sentences for each date.

Model: Le 3 décembre 1969, j'arrive au monde.

1. _____

2. _____

3. _____

4. _____

5. _____

(2) Still using the "historical present," recount something that happened in Paris on three significant dates. (Encyclopedias give information about Paris. . .)

Model: On attaque la Bastille le 14 juillet 1789.

1. _____

2. _____

3. _____

Nom _____ Cours _____ Section_____

Chapitre Cinq

A. *Cassette.* Listen first, then listen and repeat. Remember, the English equivalents are given here to help you understand <u>in general</u> the content of the dialogues. Do not copy those 'translations' into your textbook. You'll find the text of the dialogue, in French, in your textbook.

Narrator:	*A group of tourists in Paris. They are fascinated by the explanations given by their guide.*
The Guide:	You are now on the square in front of Notre-Dame. Please look at the cathedral. It is a good example of Gothic architecture.
Mme Bonpoids:	Excuse me, how old is this cathedral? Fifty years old?
The Guide:	Er . . . no! It's a bit older than that. This cathedral was built from the twelfth to the fourteenth centuries. It is therefore about 700 years old.
M. Bonpoids:	Yes, yes, I know, it's from the time of Louis XIV. He constructed this cathedral.
The Guide:	I'm terribly sorry, sir, but you are mistaken. Louis XIV was the so-called "Sun King." He lived in the seventeenth century.
Mlle Chanel:	Yes, and he built the Louvre, didn't he?
The Guide:	No, the château de Versailles. The Louvre dates from the twelfth century. It was, however, the royal residence and several kings lived in the Louvre: Henry IV, Louis XIII, and Louis XIV when he was a child.
M. Chardin:	Yes, but today the Louvre is a museum. Now where does the king of France live?
The Guide:	(exasperated) France is no longer a kingdom; we had a revolution in 1789 and we are a republic, with a president!

(The guide leaves his group of tourists, and goes off singing La Marseillaise.*)*

B. *Cassette.* Review of basic expressions and constructions. You're going to hear a series of questions and answers. As the model shows, each set will first have one pair that you are to repeat, then have a second pair in which you are to respond to the question (no "correct" answer will be given on tape as there will often be more than one possibility.)
We give reference numbers to the page in which the construction is introduced, but please try to do this exercise first <u>without</u> looking anything up.

Models: (Chap. 1-C)
a. Répétez.   -- Et Louise, comment va-t-elle? (You repeat)
                        -- Elle va bien.   (You repeat)
b. Répondez. -- Et toi, comment vas-tu? (Listen, do not repeat.)
                        -- Je vais bien, merci, et toi?   (You give your answer.)

1. (Chap. 1-D) Repeat the *a.* set; answer the *b.* question.
2. (Chap. 1-Numerals)
3. (Chap. 2-A)
4. (Chap. 2-D, E: Note--your response must be negative.)
5. (Chap. 3-A, B: Note--your response must be negative.)
6. (Chap. 3-C, D)
7. (Chap. 3-E)
8. (Chap. 4-A)

C. *Written.* In the following exercise, give the proper form of either *vouloir*, or *pouvoir*, or *écrire*, according to the meaning of the sentence.

1. Quand il fait chaud, je ne _____ pas étudier.

2. Nous _____ des lettres à nos amis.

3. C'est vendredi soir et mes amis _____ sortir. Moi, je vais rester ici et travailler.

4. _____-vous avec un crayon ou un stylo?_____

5. -- _____-vous encore du café?

    -- Non, merci.

6. Si tu_____, tu _____

D. *Written.*
    (1) Tell us what the following people/animals <u>can</u> do.

a. Je _____.

b. Mes amis _____.

c. Mon chien _____.

    (2) Tell us what the following people <u>want</u> to do.

a. Je _____.

b. Mes amis et moi _____.

c. Mon professeur _____.

E. *Written.* Give the weather expression that corresponds to the sketch. Of course, there may be more than one possible appropriate response, . . . so we give the same sketch more than once. You, on the other hand, are not permitted to repeat an expression: it's a teacher's world.

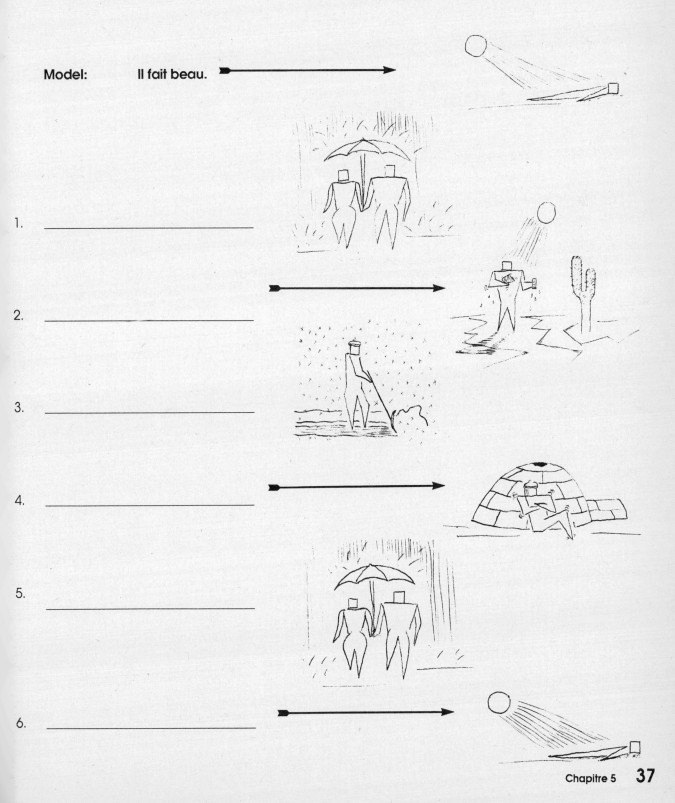

Model: Il fait beau.   ➡

1. _____

2. _____

3. _____

4. _____

5. _____

6. _____

F. *Cassette.* You're going to overhear a conversation between two friends. Madeleine has called François looking for sympathy: she's on vacation and the weather is terrible. She doesn't get much sympathy, but we get to hear lots of weather expressions, in contrasting statements. Listen and try to get the gist of what is said. AT THE END, repeat the weather expressions when they are given again, with pauses.

G. *Cassette.* Verb drill on the verbs *pouvoir, vouloir,* and *écrire.* As usual, repeat the model sentences, then give the correct form as the three cues are given. We will always give the correct response to the cue, but you are not to repeat that. If you have trouble, repeat the entire exercise.

H. *Written.* A simple, but dull exercise, just to be sure you have the forms of the interrogative adjective straight. Fill in the blanks with the proper form of *quel,* according to the gender and the number of the noun it goes with. To spice it up a bit, we've inserted a few new words, but you'll be able to pick up the gender from the rest of the question/response (for example, *ton* would lead you to the masculine form, *quel,* in the model).

Model: - <u>Quel</u> genou regardez-vous? - Je regarde ton genou.

1. -- _____ arbre regardez-vous? - Le grand arbre juste devant vous.
2. -- _____ heure est-il? - Il est six heures.
3. -- _____ couleurs préférez-vous? - Moi, je préfère les couleurs vives, comme le rouge.
4. -- _____ roman de Camus lisez-vous? - Je lis *La chute.*
5. -- _____ chemin prends-tu? - Je prends le chemin qui mène à la maison de grand-mère. (Red Riding Hood to the wolf.)
6. -- _____ hôtels choisissez-vous? - Je choisis toujours les petits hôtels charmants et pittoresques.

I. *Cassette.* Sound and word discrimination. Write the word(s) you hear, following the usual pattern.

/ mes - mais - ma / _____

/ êtes - était - étaient / _____

/ pouvons - pouvions - pouvait / _____

/ froid - frais - vrai / _____

J. *Cassette. Dictée*   "A very ordinary morning."

1. _____
2. _____
3. _____
4. _____
5. _____
6. _____
7. _____
8. _____
9. _____
10. _____
11. _____
12. _____
13. _____
14. " _____
15. _____

K. *Written.* Guided composition. We'll give the first words for each unit (which may be a short paragraph or just one sentence). You complete the units, using your imagination, but following the guidelines we give here. In the first one, set the framework (either simply tell us where you lived or take some other simple approach: e.g., imagine that you traveled to some other country that year; that you went to a private school that year, or ...). In the following ones, say what went on, within that framework, in each of the seasons.

1. Quand j'avais dix ans,_____

_____

_____

_____

_____

_____

_____

2. En hiver,_____
_____
_____
_____
_____
_____
_____

3. Au printemps,_____
_____
_____
_____
_____
_____
_____
_____

4. En été,_____
_____
_____
_____
_____
_____
_____

5. En automne,_____
_____
_____
_____
_____
_____
_____

Chapitre Six

A. *Cassette.* Before listening to the dialogue, quickly scan this English version of it, then read (again) the French version in your textbook. As you listen to the dialogue the first time, follow it in your textbook (in French). After that, listen to it a number of times, without looking at either version.

Narrator: Two girls, Evelyne and Stéphanie, are strolling in Paris.

Evelyne: Look, there are a lot of people in front of that bistro.

Stéphanie: What's going on? Let's go see.

Eveiyne: Oh, there's a mime! Look, he's making believe he's eating, but he has nothing in his hands.

Stéphanie: That's right: there's no table, no chair, no plate, no fork, no knife, no spoon.

Evelyne: This guy is really talented. Too bad he just finished up.

Stéphanie: And now he's passing the hat. You want to give him something?

Evelyne: Yes, I like him, I'm going to give him five francs. How about you?

Stéphanie: Not me. I prefer to spend my five francs at the bistro.

B. *Cassette.* A short drill to help you get used to the *passé composé* with *avoir* verbs. As usual in verb drills, repeat the first full sentence given to you, then give the proper substitute form according to the cue. You'll hear the correct response; do not repeat it. Three cues follow each sentence, then a new sentence.

1. J'ai étudié le français.
2. Il a fait ses devoirs.
3. Il a pris un taxi.
4. J'ai fermé la porte.

C. *Cassette.* This will help you get started on your own set of questions and responses for the continuation of *Questions et réponses*-A in class. Just listen to the sets we have recorded: it's okay to take notes but don't try to write everything down (this is not a *dictée*--simply a sample of the kinds of things you can ask and the kinds of answers that might be given.)

1. The prof thinks John is rich because he bought a Cadillac, but . . .
2. Françoise wasted her time in front of the tube (worse yet, watching DALLAS), while her friend wrote letters.
3. Not only did John-Paul work last night despite the noise in the meeting room, but he points out to his friend that he finished his homework, whereas his friend . . .

> *Glossaire*
> les actualités, le téléjournal,   *the news*
> une salle de réunions,   *a meeting room*
> vieux, vieille,   *old (masculine and feminine forms)*
> un chanteur,   *a singer*

D. *Cassette.* Like B, this is a drill on the *passé composé*, but with verbs that take *être* as the auxiliary. Same pattern: A short sentence that you repeat, then three cues in a row for you to produce a substitute sentence. We'll give the correct responses, but you are not to repeat them: if your responses do not match ours, it's better to go back and repeat the entire exercise.

1. Elle est allée à Paris.
2. Nous sommes partis ce matin.
3. Mes amis sont arrivés hier soir.
4. Il est entré dans la salle.

E. *Written.* Complete the following sentences by giving the correct *passé composé* form of the verb given in parentheses. Remember to check the *être* verb list in 6.2.1-b of the *Reference Grammar.* There should be no mistakes: all the forms can be looked up.

1. (boire)   J' _____ un coca.
2. (faire)   Ils _____ leurs devoirs.
3. (aller)   Tu _____ au Mexique.
4. (pouvoir)   Elles _____ voyager en France cet été.
5. (partir)   Je _____ à cinq heures.
6. (être)   Tu _____ malade hier?
7. (arriver)   Elles _____ à sept heures.
8. (choisir)   J' _____ ce disque.
9. (finir)   Vous _____ la leçon.
10. (regarder)   Il _____ la télé pendant quatre heures.

F. *Written.* What you (or someone else) did, when. Write ten sentences, using the *passé composé* and a time expression (clock time or something like "last night"), each one stating what you or X did at some time in the past. For the first five, use *avoir* verbs, the next five, *être* verbs, following the models.

Model: J'ai fini mes devoirs ce matin.

1. _____.
2. _____.
3. _____.
4. _____.
5. _____.

Model: Ma sœur est partie à six heures.

1. _____.
2. _____.
3. _____.
4. _____.
5. _____.

G. *Cassette.* This and the following exercise will be short verb drills, all following the same pattern: short sentence to repeat, three cues followed by pauses (you give the correct substitution), followed by the correct responses (you do not repeat the correct responses).

1. Je finis mes devoirs.
2. Les étudiants obéissent au prof.
3. Le malade choisit un médecin.

H. *Cassette.* Verb drill, as in Exercise G.

1. Je bois de l'eau.
2. Les enfants boivent du lait.
3. Les étudiants boivent de la bière.

I. *Cassette. Dictée.* (As we hear her recount her childhood, we're not surprised that Rosemarie became a travel agent.)

1. _____ ,

2. _____ ,

3. _____

4. _____ .

5. _____ .

6. _____ ,

7. _____ ,

8. _____

9. _____ , _____ , _____ . . .

10. _____ , _____   (use Arabic numerals)

11. _____ , _____ _____

12. _____

13. _____ .

14. _____ !

15. _____ .

J. *Cassette.* Word and sound discrimination. Write the word you hear.

1. / est - a - ai / _____

2. / finit - fini - finis / _____

3. / écrivez - écrivaient - écrit / _____

4. / a - es - as / _____

K. *Written.* We will give sentence beginnings, with an explanation of the context for that sentence. You complete the sentence using your imagination or personal experiences, being sure to use the tense that is called for by the forms proposed and/or by the situation.

1. (The person speaking just won the lottery. He/she tells us what he/she was doing just two days ago.)

   J'ai gagné à la Loterie Nationale aujourd'hui. Il y a deux jours, _____

   _____

   _____

   _____

2. (The person speaking has been converted recently to leading a better life. Formerly, she/he had various vices--list them; now, she/he does better things--list those.)

    Autrefois, quand j'étais une pécheresse (un pécheur), je..._____

    _____

    _____

    _____

    Maintenant que je suis converti(e), je..._____

    _____

    _____

    _____

3. (The person speaking was a famous athlete. She/he was injured last year and life has changed. You supply the sport and the details of changes in life-style.)

    Il y a deux ans, tout le monde me connaissait: ..._____

    _____

    _____

    Puis, l'été passé, j'ai eu un accident et j'ai été obligé(e) de renoncer à ma carrière.

    Maintenant,_____

    _____

    _____

    _____

4. (Make up a situation of your own. You might try using a recent event or a situation discussed in your student newspaper, but be sure to use French that you can handle. Explain the situation briefly in English, then write the details in French.)

    _____

    _____

    _____

    _____

    _____

Chapitre Sept

A. *Cassette.* The first time you listen to the dialogue, you may read the English equivalent given below (or you may read it <u>before</u> listening to the dialogue). The next few times, you should look at the text in your textbook. Finally, you should listen to the dialogue a few times with no text in front of you. If you wish to repeat (it is not necessary to do so: the dialogue's main purpose is to develop listening comprehension), you may stop your cassette--preferably using a "pause" button if you have one.

Setting:	*We are at the Museum of Science and Industry. It's the last week of classes. A class is on a field trip to the exhibition, "Repaired Man." At the exit, surrounded by his students, the professor asks them for their reactions.*
Professor:	What impressed you most about the exhibit?
Armand:	For me, it was the paradox that wars and catastrophes are at the origin of important scientific and technological developments.
Camille:	Yes. They explained, for example, how one should treat burns, poisonings and fractures.
Bertrand:	It's really something to see all the techniques that doctors use to "repair" people. Did you see those electronic prostheses?
Violaine:	Yes, not bad. Using electronics and the computer, they've found compensatory systems for handicapped people, the deaf and the blind. Some of their solutions are incredible.
Professor:	So, then, you learned something?
Students:	Yes, a lot.
Professor:	Good. Now, let's get over to the geodesic dome where we are supposed to see two movies. Our reservation is for two o'clock.
Students:	Great!

B. *Cassette.* Listen to the following sets of mini-dialogues or comments. Each one will contain one or more *avoir* expressions. Write as many as you hear, on the respective lines.

> **Model:**   **Il a faim.**   (This is what you write, after hearing:)
> Qu'est-ce qu'il a ce pauvre garçon?
> Il a faim. Il n'a pas mangé depuis deux jours.

1. _____
2. _____
3. _____
4. _____
5. _____

C. *Written.* Complete each of the following sentences with an *avoir* expression from the pool provided. Do not use any expression more than once. You will not have to use all the expressions provided.

/ ____ avoir soif ____ avoir froid ____ avoir tort ____ avoir raison
____ avoir besoin de ____ avoir faim ____ avoir chaud /

1. Jean dit que Marie _____ d'être prudente.

2. Il ne peut pas faire cela tout seul. _____ deux ou trois autres personnes.

3. Si vous _____, vous n'avez qu'à mettre un pull.

4. Quand on n'a pas assez mangé, _____.

5. Au mois de janvier, quand nous avons froid, les habitants du Brésil_____

D. *Cassette.* Verb drill for *dire.* Repeat the first short sentence given each time, then give the appropriate follow-up according to the cue, as in previous drills. We'll give the proper response each time, but will not leave time for it to be repeated. Later, you should repeat the full exercise.
(Note that we no longer sequence the drills starting with a *je-* form, and proceeding in order through the third person plural form. In addition, from now on, we'll regularly include *imparfait* and *passé composé* forms in our models, not just present tense forms.)

1. Je dis la vérité.
2. Qu'est-ce que vous disiez? *(imparfait)*
3. Tu dis qu'elle est malade?
4. Il a dit bonjour. *(passé composé)*
5. Ils disent qu'ils ont froid.

E. *Written.* Complete the blanks below with the proper form of the verb *dire.* Read the whole sentence to be sure of the tense and person-number required.

1. Je _____ toujours la vérité.

2. Au moment où l'inspecteur est arrivé, le criminel _____ qu'il n'avait pas peur des agents de police.

3. Nos étudiants _____ souvent que nous leur donnons trop de devoirs.

4. Pardon, je ne peux pas vous entendre. Qu'est-ce que vous _____ ?

F. *Written.* Answer each question, following the model. This is a fairly repetitive exercise, but it is important that you develop the use of the *futur proche*, and writing it out completely in the contexts we provide should help. Note that we give you, in parentheses, the time or time period at which the person replying intends to do whatever is asked.

> **Model:** Avez-vous fait vos devoirs? (ce soir)
> **Non, (mais) je vais faire mes devoirs ce soir.**

1. Alors, tu as écrit cette lettre? (tout de suite)

   _____

2. Paul, tes étudiants ont étudié pour l'examen? (ce week-end)

   _____

3. Marie est sortie avec Jean? (samedi prochain)

   _____

4. As-tu téléphoné à tes parents? (la semaine prochaine)

   _____

5. Avez-vous déjà visité la France? (l'année prochaine)

   _____

6. Est-ce que Françoise a voyagé en France? (cet été)

   _____

7. Henri, tu as fait ton lit? (tout de suite)

   _____

8. Le prof a expliqué cette leçon, n'est-ce pas? (demain)

   _____

G. *Cassette.* Review verb drill. Repeat the first sentence in each set (given below), then give the appropriate follow-up to the cue (not given below). We'll provide the proper response on the cassette, but there will not be time to repeat it: if you have trouble, it's better to repeat the entire exercise later. Each set has a different verb. We give in parentheses the chapter in which that verb (or the model it follows) is presented.

1. Je fais du ski nautique. (3)
2. On ne comprenait pas. (4)
3. Elle ne pouvait pas sortir. (5)
4. Les étudiants ne voulaient pas écouter le prof. (5)
5. Avez-vous obéi à l'agent? (6)

H. *Written.* Respond to the question with the same tense *(imparfait, passé composé,* or *futur proche)* and a contrary meaning. It doesn't have to be an exact opposite, just clearly different, as in the example.

Model: Tu vas sortir ce soir, n'est-ce pas?
 Non, je vais rester ici.

NB: Be sure to retain the same tense and same basic construction as is used in the question.

1. Le prof a fermé la porte, n'est-ce pas?
   _____

2. Tu vas étudier beaucoup cette année, n'est-ce pas?
   _____

3. Jean faisait toujours ses devoirs, n'est-ce pas?
   _____

4. Fifi avait froid hier soir, n'est-ce pas?
   _____

5. Il va faire du soleil demain, n'est-ce pas?
   _____

6. Elle est entrée à six heures, n'est-ce pas?
   _____

7. Tu as vendu ta maison, n'est-ce pas?
   _____

8. Nous allons commencer cet exercice maintenant, n'est-ce pas?
   _____

I. *Cassette. Dictée.*

1. _____
2. _____
3. _____
4. _____
5. _____
6. _____
7. _____
8. _____
9. _____
10. _____

11. _____

12. _____

13. _____

14. _____

J. *Cassette.* You will hear a series of mini-dialogues. After each one, write *oui* if the response you heard was logical and appropriate; write *non* if the response was inappropriate and/or illogical. (Note: We do not intentionally include grammatically incorrect sentences, although some may be so strange semantically that you will consider them as such.)

1. _____   2. _____   3. _____   4. _____

K. *Written.* Write five sentences following each model below. You are to compare how something is now with the way it was sometime in the past (first model) or how you expect it to be sometime in the future (second model). <u>You</u> choose the topic and the condition or quality.

Model a: Aujourd'hui il fait beau; hier il faisait moins beau.

1. _____
   _____

2. _____
   _____

3. _____
   _____

4. _____
   _____

5. _____
   _____

Model b: Maintenant, je suis content, mais demain je vais être plus content.

1. _____

   _____

2. _____

   _____

3. _____

   _____

4. _____

   _____

5. _____

   _____

Chapitre Huit

A. *Cassette.* We give two "dialogues" this time: the animal dialogue that appears at the beginning of the chapter and one of the fables from the *lecture* section at the end of the chapter.

1. For the dialogue, as usual, first read the loose translation to be sure you have the general content. Then play the cassette, looking at the French version in your textbook. Later, play the cassette without looking at either version. Repeat, if you wish, by stopping your cassette after each speaker finishes.

Situation: A tortoise is taking a walk. All of a sudden she is surrounded by a bunch of animals. They are farm animals.

Tortoise:	Greetings, cow! Where do you live?
Cow:	I live in the stable with the other cows, some calves and a big black bull.
Tortoise:	And what do you know how to do?
Cow:	Moo, moo! I graze and I give milk.
Tortoise:	And you, horse, what do you know how to do?
Horse:	Neigh, neigh! I know how to run, leap and jump.

The tortoise continues her walk.

Tortoise:	Hi, pigs. And you, what do you know how to do?
Pigs:	Oink, oink! We know how to roll in the mud and we stink.
Tortoise:	And you, little cat, what do you know how to do?
Cat:	Meow, meow! I hunt mice and I purr.
Dog:	And me, I bark, bow-wow!, to protect the house and chase the cats, the cows and the sheep.
Tortoise:	And you, chickens, what do you know how to do?
Chickens:	Cluck, cluck! We lay eggs and we eat grain.

The rooster comes along.

Rooster:	Cockle-doodle-doo! Cockle-doodle-doo! Me, I'm the boss, I wake everybody up in the morning.
Sheep:	Baa, baa. Me, I give wool.
Donkey:	Hee-haw! Hee-haw! Me, I pull the cart and I am stubborn.
Tortoise:	You all live together? Do you like each other?

All reply at the same time.

All:	(All the animal sounds above, plus some others, jumbled together.)

2. For the fable, we do not give a translation. The recording is done twice, once rapidly, once with pauses. Use the recording to help you as you memorize this fable.

B. *Written.* This is a simple substitution exercise: you definitely have to know the forms of the indirect object and we're providing an opportunity to practice writing them. REWRITE each sentence, replacing the indirect object by the one given in parentheses. Do not change the subject.

Model: Je te donne mon stylo. (lui)
Je lui donne mon stylo.

1. Elle me rend les devoirs. (nous)

   _____.

2. Vous m'avez parlé de Jean? (leur)

   _____?

3. Tu vas lui offrir un cadeau, n'est-ce pas? (me)

   _____?

C. *Written.* Now let's make that a bit more interesting. We'll provide just the framework of a sentence: the subject and the verb. You will fill in the indirect object pronoun (an appropriate one for the sense of the sentence) and any other necessary constructions (direct object or adverbial phrase). Go back to the vocabulary in *Intégration: 4-6* for ideas on vocabulary.

Model: Nous _____ envoyons_____.
Nous lui envoyons souvent des lettres.

1. La patronne _____ a posé _____.
2. Mon père va _____ montrer_____.
3. Ce monsieur _____ a dit: "_____"
4. Est-ce que tu _____ obéis?
5. Le professeur ne _____ a pas expliqué _____.
6. J'ai envie de _____ acheter _____.
7. Monsieur, voulez-vous bien _____ répéter _____?
8. Ma mère _____ a lu _____.
9. Cet avocat va _____ vendre _____.
10. Tu _____ plais, chéri.

D. *Cassette.* Now let's do some simple substitutions with the books closed, responding to oral cues. We'll give a sentence containing an indirect pronoun, then give (in a different voice) a different indirect object pronoun. You restate the sentence, substituting the new pronoun for the one in the original sentence. (Your model is all of *Exercice B.*) We'll give the proper response in each case, but do not want you to repeat it. If you have trouble, it's better to repeat the whole exercise, paying careful attention each time to the proper responses as they are given.

E. *Cassette.* The following is a familiar question-answer exercise. Please be sure that you use the appropriate pronouns in your response: see the model sentences.

> **Models:** **a.** Tu veux me parler?
> -- Oui, je veux te parler.
> **b.** Je vous ai donné une bonne note, n'est-ce pas?
> -- Oui, vous m'avez donné une bonne note.

F. *Cassette.* Complete the blanks with the proper form of the verb *savoir* or *connaître*, according to the meaning of the sentence.

1. Je _____ que Budapest est la capitale de la Hongrie.

2. Très bien. Est-ce que tu _____ Budapest?

3. Non, je ne l'ai jamais visitée, mais je_____qu'elle est sur le Danube.

4. Formidable! Dis, tu_____mon amie, Josée? Elle aussi s'intéresse
   à la géographie.

5. Josée Dupuis? Oui, j'ai fait sa connaissance hier, mais je ne _____
   pas que tu la _____.

6. Oh! si. Nous sommes allés au même lycée ici à Paris. C'est pourquoi nous
   _____ si bien la ville.

G. *Cassette.* Verb drill on *savoir* and *connaître.* Usual pattern.

H. *Written.* Working with the pool of verbs given below, complete the blanks in the sentences by writing the imperative of a verb that "fits" (right meaning), along with an appropriate indirect object pronoun to fill out the command.

Model: _____mon livre.
Rends-moi mon livre.
N.B. Don't use any verb more than once.

/___ rendre   ___ donner   ___ dire   ___ expliquer   ___ chanter
        ___ parler   ___ être /

1. _____ la vérité.

2. _____ une autre chanson.

3. _____ d'amour.

4. _____ de bonnes notes, s'il vous plaît.

5. Ne_____ pas le problème.

6. _____ sa carte d'identité.

I. *Written.* Fill in the blank with the proper form of *offrir* or *ouvrir*, according to the meaning of the sentence.

1. Quand j'ai chaud, j'_____ la fenêtre.

2. La porte est fermée, n'est-ce pas? Non, elle est_____.

3. Elle m'_____ un cadeau magnifique chaque année.

4. Nous vous_____ le choix entre la liberté et la mort.

5. Ces étudiants_____ des milliers de boîtes de bière.

J. *Cassette.* Verb drill on *ouvrir* and *offrir*. Usual pattern.

K. *Cassette.* Sound/word discrimination. Write out the word(s) that you hear.

1. / offrir - ouvrir - ouvrez / _____

2. / ouvert - va faire - offert / _____

3. / c'est - sais - sait - ces / _____

4. / deux - de - du / _____

5. / sur - su - sous / _____

L. *Cassette.* Dictée.

1. _____.

2. _____.

3. _____.

4. _____.

5. _____. *(Ils l'ont...)*

6. _____.

7. _____.

8. _____.

9. _____.

10. _____.

11. _____.

12. _____.

13. _____.

14. _____.

M. *Written.* Composition. Write six different very short paragraphs, following closely the model below. We want you to take time to choose the people you're going to mention (friends, relatives, public figures, imaginary people), then follow the framework of the model in an imaginative way.

Model: Voilà mon professeur de français. C'est un homme très pauvre. Je vais lui donner 5.000 dollars. (et il va me donner une bonne note?)

You don't have to add a comment in parentheses, but it might be amusing.

1. _____
   _____
   _____
   _____
   _____
   _____
   _____

2. _____
   _____
   _____
   _____
   _____
   _____
   _____

3. _____
   _____
   _____
   _____
   _____
   _____
   _____

4. _____

_____

_____

_____

_____

_____

5. _____

_____

_____

_____

_____

_____

Chapitre Neuf

A. *Cassette.* Follow the established pattern in working with the recorded dialogue. Please don't break that pattern. It is important that you know, in general, what is being said, but we don't want you to focus explicitly on each separate word and grammatical construction. If you repeat, try to imitate the speakers completely; imagine the situation and, when appropriate, use gestures. Whether or not you choose to repeat (your instructor may, of course, tell you to do so), we strongly urge you simply to listen to the recording several times in addition (at various intervals).

The setting: *Some French students introduce themselves to you and tell you about their plans for the future.*

Marc: I've just finished my *lycée* studies. I earned a Math degree. I'd like to become a doctor. Medical studies are in three cycles in France. The first cycle is entirely devoted to basic sciences and lasts two years. But before going into the second year, I must win in a very selective competition. You have to figure four years for the second cycle, and the third one may take anywhere from two to four years. The lenghth of that last one will depend on my specialization.

Viviane: Me, I'd like to become a technician but I don't want to get involved in a long course of study. That's why I am applying for one of the University Institutes of Technology, since the length of study at those places is only two years.

Anna: Like Marc, I have my *bac,* and I'm now in my first cycle at the university, which lasts two years. At the end I'll earn a Diploma in General University Studies. As a specialization, I'm going to choose economics. My brother, on the other hand, is working for a Diploma in Scientific and Technical University Studies, because he wants to get into computer science.

Christian: I've just been accepted in the CPGE, which is a course of study preparatory to entering the so-called *"grandes écoles."* For two years, they prepare us for the entrance exams held for each of those schools. The one I want to get into is the *Ecole normale supérieure.*

B. *Written.* Adverb formation. Quick and easy exercise, but a good chance to develop your vocabulary in both adjectives and adverbs. We give the masculine singular form of an adjective: you give the feminine singular, then the adverb that is derived from that adjective. *NB:* When the adverb is not formed from the feminine singular form, we mark it with an asterisk.

1. vrai _____ * _____
2. lent _____ _____
3. joli _____ * _____
4. complet _____ _____
5. joyeux _____ _____
6. sévère _____ _____
7. certain _____ _____
8. long _____ _____
9. naturel _____ _____
10. fréquent _____ * _____

C. *Cassette.* Word recognition. You will hear a set of eight sentences, each containing at least one adverb. Write the adverb(s) you hear on the corresponding line (line numbers will be given on the cassette).

1. _____   5. _____
2. _____   6. _____
3. _____   7. _____
4. _____   8. _____

D. *Written.* Complete the blanks with the proper form of the verb *lire.*

1. Marie _____ au lit tous les soirs avant de s'endormir.

2. Un soir, elle _____ un roman de Gide quand Philippe lui a téléphoné pour voir si elle voulait sortir.

3. Quand elle lui a dit ce qu'elle faisait, il a répondu: "Moi, j'_____ ce roman la semaine passée."

4. On a parlé un peu et elle a dit: "Tu sais, nous_____souvent les mêmes romans."

5. Maintenant, ils_____ensemble avant de se coucher: ils sont mariés.

E. *Cassette.* Verb drill for *lire*. Usual pattern. Pay attention to the tense that is used in the model sentence for each set.

1. Je lis *Paris Match.*
2. Elle a lu le jounal.
3. Nous lisions des lettres.

F. *Written.* Jean-Paul is a generalist, a jack-of-all-trades, a "Renaissance" man, . . . Philippe, on the other hand, has a one-track mind, thinks small, does not try to do too many things. Give Philippe's response to Jean-Paul's statements, following the model.

Model: Jean-Paul: Je parle français. Je parle espagnol. Je parle chinois.
Philippe: **Moi, je ne parle que le français.**

1. Je lis des romans. Je lis des pièces. Je lis des poèmes.
   _____.

2. Je sais danser. Je sais chanter. Je sais jouer du piano.
   _____.

3. Je fais du ski alpin. Je fais du ski nautique. Je fais de la natation.
   _____.

4. Je suis riche. Je suis intelligent. Je suis célèbre.
   _____.

5. J'ai voyagé en Europe. J'ai voyagé en Asie. J'ai voyagé en Afrique.
   _____.

G. *Cassette.* We'll provide a cue sentence that indicates that someone <u>does</u> or <u>has</u> only a specific subset of something. You respond, using the construction, *"ne...que,"* as in the model.

Model: Tu fais tes devoirs ce soir, et tu ne fais rien d'autre?
--C'est ça. Je ne fais que mes devoirs ce soir.

H. *Written.* Complete the blanks with the proper form of the verb *dormir.*

1. Étudiant: Je _____ bien quand je travaille bien.
2. Prof: Ah, oui? Alors vous n'allez pas bien_____ce soir.
3. Étudiant: Pourquoi pas?
   Prof: Parce que vous_____en classe aujourd'hui au lieu de travailler.
4. Étudiant: Oui, c'est vrai. Nous_____tous dans votre cours, monsieur. Mais je vais travailler ce soir.
5. Prof: (turning to the other students) Qui_____jusqu'à neuf heures ce matin?

I. *Cassette.* Drill on the verb *dormir.* Same pattern as usual.

1. On dort bien quand il fait froid.
2. Nous avons dormi huit heures.
3. Ils dormaient quand je suis entré.

J. *Written.* We give a sentence containing a reflexive verb in the *passé composé.* You rewrite (completely rewrite) the sentence twice, once in the present tense, once in the *futur proche.* Be sure to change any time expressions to fit the tense; add one if you wish to make a sentence more natural.

Model: Elle s'est couchée à minuit hier soir.
Elle se couche toujours à minuit.
Elle va se coucher ce soir à minuit.

1. Nous nous sommes levés de bonne heure aujourd'hui.

   _____ .

   _____ .

2. Je me suis lavé les mains.

   _____ .

   _____ .

3. Tu t'es bien amusée hier soir?

   _____ .

   _____ .

4. Il s'en est allé la semaine dernière.

   _____ .

   _____ .

5. Ils se sont dépêchés.

   _____ .

   _____ .

Nom _____ Cours _____ Section_____

K. *Cassette. Dictée.*

_____.

_____.

_____.

_____.

_____Comédiens de l'Épervier,

_____

_____.

"Le_____malgré_____".

_____

_____

_____

_____Sganarelle.

L. *Cassette. Aural Comprehension.* You'll hear a sentence, followed by three completion phrases or sentences, each labled "a" or "b" or "c". Write the letter corresponding to the best, most appropriate completion or response to the sentence.

1. _____   2. _____   3. _____

M. *Written.* Composition. The police are holding you on suspicion of burglarizing a university office. The burglary occurred early yesterday morning and someone claims to have seen you near the building at 6 a.m. Your roommate has confirmed your absence from the room when he or she woke up at 5:45. Tell the police what you did from 3 a.m. to 7 a.m. yesterday. (They want the facts; <u>we</u> want at least three reflexive verbs.)

_____

_____

_____

_____

_____

_____

_____

_____

_____

_____

_____

_____

_____

_____

That should be enough space in which to prove you are innocent. If you're going to say anymore, get a lawyer who speaks French.

Chapitre Dix

A. *Cassette.*   As usual, the dialogue will be read twice. Read the English version here first, just for the sense of it. Then listen to the dialogue, trying to imagine what is happening. Look at the French text (in your textbook) the first time, but then listen to it (frequently) without looking at either text. You may stop the cassette and repeat, if you wish to do so.

It is morning. Imagine four girls, Denise, Zéon, Liliane, and Marie-Claude. They share an apartment. Unfortunately, there is only one bathroom.

Marie-Claude: Is the bathroom free?

Zénon: No, you see perfectly well that I'm getting washed.

Marie-Claude: Hurry up. I want to wash my hair this morning and I've got an appointment with Jean-Paul Belmondo in an hour.

Zénon: I'm not leaving here until I've put on my makeup, and I want to add some blue to my hair, because, me, I've got a date with Alain Delon in fifty minutes.

Denise: *(comes running up)* Watch out. Let me by. I'm late. My plane takes off in forty minutes.

Marie-Claude: Your alarm clock didn't work?

Denise: Yes, but I went back to sleep.

Liliane: *(walks in yawning)* What is this "circus"? Me too, I'm in a hurry. I've got an appointment with the Prime Minister in a half-hour. Denise, where are you flying to?

Denise: I'm leaving for... I forgot. Marie-Claude, where am I going?

Marie-Claude: Yesterday, you told me that you were going to Morocco.

Denise: Well, then, that's it. I'm going to Morocco. Or is it Japan?

Liliane: Make up your mind. Have you already bought your ticket?

Denise: No, and I haven't even packed. Hurry up everybody, I want to take a shower!

Zénon: Calm down. Even if you took a taxi to the airport . . . you know it's already nine-thirty. In short: you've missed your plane; and in any case, despite your story, you're not going to get ahead of us.

B. *Written.* Rewrite the following sentences (completely!), substituting direct object pronouns for the underlined direct objects.

Model: Jean ferme <u>la porte</u>.
           Jean **la** ferme.

1. Je vois <u>les enfants</u>.

   _____.

2. Elle va chercher <u>son livre</u>.

   _____.

3. Nous chantions <u>ces chansons</u>.

   _____.

4. Elles ont compris <u>la question</u>.

   _____.

5. Il ne veut pas regarder <u>ce film</u>.

   _____.

6. Je n'ai pas donné <u>mes clés</u> à Fifi.

   _____.

7. Nous allons voir <u>le film "États d'âme"</u>.

   _____.

8. Tu as vu <u>les Jeux Olympiques</u> à la télé?

   _____?

C. *Cassette.* Answer the questions, replacing nouns with pronouns as you would in natural conversation. In some cases, there will be no nouns to replace, but it will be necessary--in order to make sense--to switch pronouns (see the model).

Model: Tu as trouvé mes clés?
           --Oui, je les ai trouvées.

         Vous m'avez entendu, n'est-ce pas?
           --Oui, je vous ai entendu(e)

D. *Written.* Answer the following questions, replacing nouns by pronouns and adding your own words as necessary to give a complete answer.

Model: À qui vas-tu donner cette mauvaise note?
--Je vais la donner à ce mauvais étudiant.

1. Quand avez-vous fini vos devoirs?

   _____.

2. À qui a-t-elle offert son cœur?

   _____.

3. Où a-t-on trouvé le lion?

   _____.

4. As-tu vu ton prof hier soir?

   _____.

5. À qui allez-vous raconter cette histoire?

   _____.

E. *Written.* To complete each blank choose a verb from the following "pool," according to the context of the sentence, and give the appropriate form of that verb (tense, person-number). Do not use any verb more than once. (*Note:* These are all "regular" *-re* verbs.)

/_____ vendre   _____ perdre   _____ attendre   _____ entendre   _____ répondre /

1. Notre équipe _____ le match de basket-ball hier soir.
2. Est-ce qu'on _____ du jambon à la charcuterie?
3. (un étudiant, agité...): Mais, monsieur, _____ toujours à vos questions et vous dites maintenant que je ne faisais pas attention en classe. Ce n'est pas juste!
4. À cette université, les étudiants _____ les profs qui sont en retard jusqu'à la fin du cours.
5. Pardon? Que dis-tu? Je ne peux pas t' _____.

F. *Cassette.* Drill on the verb *vendre*.

G. *Written.* Complete the blanks with the proper form of the verb *voir*.

1. Regarde ce journal. Qu'est-ce que tu _____?
2. Ils _____ le premier ministre hier devant la cathédrale.
3. Je vais _____ si on peut entrer un peu avant les autres.
4. Je n'aime pas ces lunettes. Je _____ mieux avec mes anciennes lunettes.
5. Vous _____ cet homme là-bas? C'est un espion.

H. *Cassette.* Drill on the verb *voir.*

I. *Cassette.* Word and sound discrimination. Rewrite, in the space provided, the word or phrase that you hear.

1. / allé - aller - allez - allais / _____

2. / aimé - aimer - aimez - aimait / _____

3. / entendre - attendre / _____

4. / elles ont - elles sont / _____

5. / vous - vu - veut / _____

J. *Cassette. Dictée.*

1. _____ .

2. _____ .

3. _____ .

4. _____ .

5. _____ , *Paris-Match,*

6. _____ :

7. _____

8. _____ .

9. _____

10. _____ .

11. _____ . . .

12. _____ .

K. *Written.* Using the verb tables as necessary, write the infinitive of each underlined verb fom in the space provided. All of the underlined verbs are in the *passé simple*, the "literary" or "book" tense. See the *Reference Grammar,* 6.2.3.

1. Ils <u>vinrent</u> tout de suite. _____

2. On <u>alla</u> à Constantinople. _____

3. Napoléon <u>fit</u> quatre pas vers lui. _____

4. Elle <u>eut</u> peur. _____

5. Le Petit Prince ne <u>dit</u> rien. _____

6. Nous <u>marchames</u> jusqu'à la frontière. _____

7. L'enfant <u>se mit</u> à pleurer. _____

8. Personne ne <u>fut</u> là. _____

L. *Written.* Complete each "paragraph" that we start for you by writing three sentences-one referring to the past, one to the present, one to the future- all about the item (person or thing) mentioned by us. FOLLOW THE MODEL, using direct object pronouns

Model: Voici mon stylo. **Je l'ai acheté à la librairie. Je l'emploie pour écrire mes devoirs. Je vais le garder toujours.**

1. Voilà ma voiture. _____
   _____
   _____

2. Voilà la maison de mon professeur. _____
   _____
   _____

3. Voici mon livre de français. _____
   _____
   _____

4. Voilà mon meilleur ami. / Voilà ma meilleure amie. (Rayer la mention inutile.) _____
   _____
   _____
   _____

5. Voilà (name a well-known, living, person)... _____
   _____
   _____
   _____

Chapitre Onze

A. *Cassette.* The following are loose translations of the dialogues in your textbook. Read them quickly before listening to the cassette, just to be sure you know what each one is about. <u>Do</u> <u>not</u> write the translations in your textbook.

At the "kiosque"

Passerby:	Give me a *télécarte*, please.
Owner/Manager:	Do you want a small one or a large one?
Passerby:	What's the difference?
Owner/Manager:	On the little one you get 50 units, on the big one you get about 300.
Passerby:	I'll take the little one. How much?
Owner/Manager:	Forty francs.

At the "Gare de Lyon"

A passerby wants to go to the suburbs. She stops at the métro ticket window.

Passerby: A ticket for Park St.-Maur and a packet of tickets, please.

She hands the cashier a twenty-franc bill.

Cashier: That's not enough! It comes to thirty-six francs. Do you have another twenty-franc note?

Passerby: Oh, excuse me, I mixed up a bill for twenty with a bill for a hundred.

In front of the "Halles" shopping center

Young man: Excuse me, ma'am, would you mind participating in a poll?

Woman: I can't. I'm not from around here.

Young man: True enough. Tourists don't count. Too bad.

At a sidewalk café

A young couple has just sat down at a table.

Waiter: What would you like?

Young man: Two coffees, one small, one large.

Waiter: With a *croissant*?

Both: Yes, please.

B. *Written.* Regardez l'arbre généalogique et répondez aux questions.

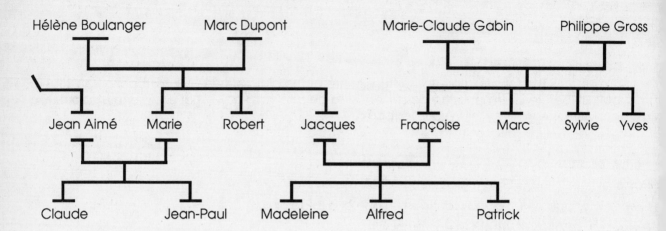

1. Les parents de Marie, Robert et Jacques sont Monsieur et Madame Dupont. Quel était le nom de jeune fille de Madame Dupont? C'était _____.

2. Quel était le nom de jeune fille de la mère de Françoise, Marc, Sylvie et Yves? _____ _____.

3. Nommez la cousine de Claude. _____.

4. Qui est la belle-mère de Jean Aimé? _____.

5. Savez-vous qui est la belle-mère de Marie Aimé, née Dupont? _____ _____.

6. a. Qui est le grand-père maternel de Patrick Dupont? _____

   b. Et qui est son grand-père paternel? _____.

7. Robert Dupont n'a pas d'enfants, mais il a des neveux et une nièce. Comment s'appellent-ils (noms complets, s'il vous plaît) ? _____ _____.

8. Quelles[1] sont les tantes de Madeleine Dupont? _____ _____.

---

1. Recall that the interrogative pronoun/adjective, when used wth the verb *être* as it is here, will regularly mean "who" when the expression on the other side of the verb "to be" refers to a person or persons. In such cases, it is more common to use *quel* than to use *qui*, but you need not worry about the choice at this point in your career.

C. *Cassette.* Substitution drill. Repeat each short sentence, replacing the appropriate word or words with the expression given immediately after the sentence, as in the model. Note: make all necessary additional changes. We give the most likely answers; others are possible in some cases.

Model: Je parle à Jean. (à personne)
Je ne parle à personne.

D. *Written.* Answer the following questions in the negative, without using *pas.* We'll underline the expression that should be negated.

Model: Quand vas-tu finir cet exercice.
Je ne vais jamais finir cet exercice.
OR, better: **Je ne vais jamais le finir.**

1. Qui a écrit ce conte philosophique?

   _____.

2. À qui parlais-tu quand je suis entrée?

   _____.

3. Avez-vous jamais vu cette pièce musicale?

   _____.

4. Tu fais souvent tes devoirs en classe?

   _____.

5. Qui cherches-tu?

   _____.

6. Qu'est-ce que tu vas faire ce soir?

   _____.

7. Que regardez-vous?

   _____.

8. Marie sort toujours avec Jean-Paul?

   _____.

9. Qui va t'accompagner au théâtre?

   _____.

10. Qu'est-ce que vous avez envoyé au président?

    _____.

E. *Written.* Complete the blanks with the appropriate form for the verb *tenir* or *venir,* according to the context. Read the entire dialogue before answering.

1. -- Est-ce que tu _____ absolument à rester ici jusqu'à demain?

2. -- Bien sûr. Je _____ ici hier pour voir Henri et je ne vais pas partir avant son retour.

3. --Mais comment savez-vous qu'il va _____ ici demain?

4. --Parce que je t'ai entendu au téléphone ce matin et tu as dit: "Alors, Henri, tu _____ _____ demain?" C'était clair que sa réponse était affirmative.

5. -- _____! Tu écoutes les conversations privées?

6. --Pas d'habitude.

F. *Cassette.* Verb drill on *venir* and *tenir.*

G. *Written.* Simple transformation exercises. Your roommate, Jean, tells you he's going to do something. You respond that you've just done that very thing.

Model: Jean: Tu sais, je vais écrire une lettre à mes parents.
Vous: **Moi, je viens d'écrire une lettre à ma mère.**

1. Jean: Je vais faire mes devoirs.
   Vous: Tiens, _____.

2. Jean: Je vais téléphoner à Marie.
   Vous: Elle n'est pas là. _____.

3. Jean: Je vais laver la voiture.
   Vous: Ce n'est pas la peine. _____.

4. Jean: J'ai froid. Je vais fermer la fenêtre.
   Vous: Tu n'as pas vu? _____.

H. *Cassette.* Substitution drills with *venir de.* Follow the instructions on the cassette, replacing the subject or the object as indicated.

I. *Cassette.* Word and sound discrimination. Rewrite the word(s) that you hear.

1. / de   du   des /   _____

2. / le   la   lu /   _____

3. / l'ai   la   les /   _____

4. / ils sont   ils ont   ils vont /   _____

J. *Cassette.* Laquelle est la bonne réponse: *a*, ou *b*, ou *c*?

1. _____   2. _____   3. _____

K. *Cassette. Dictée.*

1. _____
2. _____.
3. _____.
4. _____.
5. _____, _____.
6. _____
7. _____
8. _____.
9. _____
10. _____
11. _____.
12. _____
13. _____.

L. *Written.* Write a dialogue between two small children who speak French amazingly well and who have been told to use the expressions introduced in this chapter: the various negatives, the verbs *tenir* and *venir,* and the idiomatic "immediate past" tense using *venir de* + INFINITIVE. The children are Claude and Jean-Paul Aimé (see written exercise B), and they might discuss their cousins and other relatives as well as any other topic you feel they (you) can handle. Look at the vocabulary lists for ideas. At least ten lines.

_____

_____

_____

_____

_____

_____

_____

_____

_____

_____

_____

_____

_____

_____

Chapitre Douze

A. *Cassette.* Quickly scan the following version, in English, of the interview that is given to you in the text. Then listen to the recording of the interview a number of times, preferably without the text in front of you. As usual, you may use the pause or stop button and repeat if you wish, but this is principally for comprehension.

Louise: What is your name, and where do you come from?

Famaria: My name is Famaria Koné. I'm from the Republic of the Ivory Coast in West Africa. I'm from Abidjan; I went to school there and my parents still live there.

Louise: What is Abidjan like?

Famaria: Abidjan is not very different from most large cities in America or in Europe. We have large buildings and an infrastructure that one usually finds in this kind of city. However, there are still some things that are unique to the Ivory Coast, stemming from the traditionalism that we try to preserve.

Louise: Could you give me an example?

Famaria: Yes. For example, the suit, that is: pants, shirt and tie and jacket, is considered the official men's apparel in Europe. That's about the same in the Ivory Coast, except that one will find as well the traditional noble costume, which consists of a pair of trousers, a shirt and a *grand boubou*, a *chichia*, (a kind of hat) and sandals (*babouches*).

Louise: What's the role of the family?

Famaria: Myself, I'm very attached to my family and we try to see each other often. The ties to my family are very strong. We also have very close ties with our neighbors; we help each other all the time.

Louise: What do you do for entertainment or relaxation in Abidjan?

Famaria: As for leisure activities, you can do almost anything. Abidjan is a very developed city. You find everything there.

Louise: What do you think of your country?

Famaria: The Ivory Coast is beautiful. It's an interesting country to visit. It's a country that is open to the future, but which does not want to forget its past. To know where one is going, it's necessary to know where one comes from.

B. *Written.*   Rewrite each sentence, replacing the underlined noun by the one given in parentheses. Make all necessary changes. (See the *Reference Grammar*, 2.4.1 and 2.4.2.)

Model: <u>Marie</u> est sportive. (Jacques)
   Jacques est sportif.

1.   C'est un long <u>roman</u> .   (pièce)

   _____.

2.   J'ai loué un petit <u>appartement</u> .   (maison)

   _____.

3.   C'est un <u>chat</u> noir.   (porte)

   _____.

4.   C'est une belle <u>église</u> .   (château)

   _____.

5.   C'est un beau <u>bâtiment</u> .   (hôtel)

   _____.

6.   Tous les <u>garçons</u> sont absents.   (jeunes filles)

   _____.

7.   Cet <u>étudiant</u> est paresseux.   (étudiante)

   _____.

8.   Mon <u>ami</u> est très gentil.   (amie)

   _____.

C.   *Written.*   Complete the blank with the form of *partir* or *sortir* that is required by the context.

1.   Elle _____ avec Jean hier soir.

2.   Le _____ dans cinq minutes.

3.   -- Jacques, appelez-nous un taxi: nous _____ pour l'aéroport.

4.   Quand il avait dix-huit ans, il _____ tous les week-ends avec ses
   copains.

5.   -- Est-ce que les Dupont vont partir ce soir?

   -- Les Dupont? Ils _____ hier!

6.   --Où est Michel?

   -- Il _____ la voiture du garage.

D.   *Cassette.*   Verb drill on *partir* and *sortir*.

E. *Written.* We'll provide a list of colors. You think of something that is usually that color, then write a sentence. You are free to use more than one color in a sentence (as in describing a flag), and you are not required to use all of them--but don't use the same one over and over, please!

Model: (one of the colors given is: *rouge*)
Les tomates sont bonnes quand elles sont rouges.

/ les couleurs: rouge, blanc, noir, violet, brun, rose, gris, vert, bleu, orange, jaune, pourpre /

1. _____
2. _____
3. _____
4. _____
5. _____
6. _____
7. _____
8. _____

F. *Cassette.* Answer the question, using the geographical location given as a cue.

Model: Où allez-vous l'année prochaine? (...France)
Nous allons en France.

G. *Cassette.* Review of cardinal numerals. Write the number you hear in each sentence or mini-dialogue. Write just the number, in Arabic numerals.

1. _____
2. _____
3. _____
4. _____
5. _____
6. _____
7. _____
8. _____
9. _____
10. _____

H. *Written.* Ordinal numerals and adjectives. Think of a class of objects/persons, such as "students" or "cars". Then imagine that there are six of them in a row. Describe each one in order. (For example, if you choose cars, you might say: *La première voiture est bleue.*)

1. _____.
2. _____.
3. _____.
4. _____.
5. _____.
6. _____.

I. *Cassette. Dictée.*

1. _____.
2. _____,
3. _____.
4. _____.
5. _____.
6. _____.
7. _____.
8. _____.
9. _____.

J. *Cassette.* Aural comprehension. Indicate whether the response in each of the following mini-dialogues is logical and appropriate or not. If it is, write *oui;* if not, write *non.*

1. _____ 2. _____ 3. _____ 4. _____

Chapitre Treize

A. *Cassette.* Read this English version of the dialogue in your text, then listen to the cassette recording. As usual, we do not leave time for repetition: we want you to concentrate on listening and on imagining the situation.

Madame Vincent, the assistant director of the "Euro-monde" Travel Agency, is interviewing a young man, M. Michelin, who is interested in a job with her agency.

An employee: Ms Vincent, this is Alain Michelin. He's replying to the ad in the paper.

Mme Vincent: Good. Please come in. Have a seat.

M. Michelin: Thank you.

Mme Vincent: Tell me a little about your work experience. Have you ever worked for a travel agency?

M. Michelin: Yes, I worked for two years for *Euro-tour.* I liked it very much. I had the chance to travel just about everywhere in Europe. Obviously, I mainly visited Western countries with our clients, but I also organized several tours to Eastern bloc nations: Poland, Hungary, Bulgaria . . . .

Mme Vincent: Then why do you want to change jobs and come work for us?

M. Michelin: My agency only takes groups to places in Europe. But I'd like to see other things: Australia, the United States, South America, ...

Mme Vincent: (cutting him short) Thank you, Mr. Michelin. We will inform you of our decision within two weeks. Good luck.

M. Michelin: Goodbye Ms Vincent. I hope to be working for you soon.

B. *Written.* Answer the following questions, using the future tense as in the model. Add an appropriate adverb or adverbial phrase, at least in a few of the sentences. (Some of the questions will also be in the future tense.)

Model: As-tu fini tes devoirs?
   Non, mais je les finirai ce soir.

1. Sont-ils déjà partis?

   _____.

2. Quand viendra-t-il à Paris?

   _____.

3. Où passeront-ils leurs vacances de Noël?

   _____.

4. Tu es prête à partir Michèle?

   Non, mais _____.

5. Pouvez-vous nous aider maintenant?

   _____.

6. Est-ce qu'il est allé en France l'année passée?

   Non, mais _____.

C. *Cassette.* Drill on verb forms in the future tense. Same format as for irregular verbs. Repeat the model sentence, then supply the correct response to each cue (we give a new subject, you insert that and make all necessary changes).

Two hints on pronunciation: for *-ir* verbs, like *finir*, be sure to pronounce the *i* before the *r* clearly: American students have a tendency to "reduce" that vowel; on the other hand, be careful to pronounce the *e* in *ferai, fera*, etc. as a "schwa" (reduced vowel), not as an /e/ or /ɛ/.

D. *Written.* We are going to supply an answer. Your task is to compose a question that could have elicited that answer, with a focus on the underlined portion. Your questions should all be "info" questions, not "yes/no" questions, and all should involve an interrogative adverb. If we give an expression in parentheses, use it to "flesh out" your question.

Model: We give: Je les ferai <u>à six heures</u> .   (devoirs)
You write: **Quand ferez-vous vos devoirs?**

1. _____?

   -- Il habite <u>à Alger</u> .   (Meursault)

2. _____?

   -- Elle <u>va beaucoup mieux</u> , merci.   (fille)

3. _____?

   -- <u>Parce que je les déteste</u> .   (ne pas manger. . . haricots verts)

4. _____?

   -- J'irai <u>à Paris et à Rome</u> .   (l'été prochain)

5. _____?

   -- Elle <u>a pris l'autocar</u> .   (ta femme . . . aller à Nîmes)

6. _____?

   -- Je l'ai trouvé <u>au marché aux puces</u> .   (chapeau + ADJ)

E. *Cassette.* Verb drill on *servir.* Usual pattern.

F. *Written.* Answer the following questions, following the model. Please try to do this first without looking anything up. It's a test of your vocabulary.

Model: À quoi sert un stylo?
Un stylo sert à écrire.

1. À quoi sert un professeur?

   _____.

2. À quoi sert un couteau?

   _____.

3. À quoi sert un livre?

   _____.

4. À quoi sert un réveil (un réveille-matin) ?

   _____.

5. À quoi sert le parfum?

   _____.

G. *Written.* Fill in the blanks with the appropriate form of the tonic (stressed, disjunctive) pronoun. In some cases, there will be more than one possible answer.

Model: Louise et ___**moi**___ , nous allons au cinéma ce soir.

1. _____, je n'y comprends rien!

2. -- Qui est à la porte?

    --_____.   (the person at the door is responding)

3. --Tu connais les Brouillon?

    --Oui, en effet, je vais dîner chez _____ demain soir.

4. --Tu vas voir Paul ce week-end?

    --Oui, je vais avec _____ au concert *rock* .

5. --Pour qui as-tu acheté ces fleurs?

    --Mais, pour _____, ma chérie.

6. --Est-ce que Jean a pu parler avec les chanteuses?

    --Oui, il était assis à côté d' _____.

H. *Cassette.* A quick review drill of the tonic pronouns. Same pattern as for verb drills, but you just change the tonic pronoun according to the cue.

I. *Cassette.* Word and sound discrimination.

1. / auront - aurons - sauront - saurons /   _____

2. / acheté - acheter - achetez - achetait /   _____

3. / bon - bonne /   _____

J. *Cassette. Dictée.*

1. _____ .
2. _____
3. _____
4. _____
5. _____ .
6. _____
7. _____ .
8. _____ ,
9. _____
10. _____ .

K. *Written.* You have arrived late for class. It's late in the semester and your instructor insists that you give your excuse in French. Do so, being sure to be imaginative and to use a few difficult constructions so as to impress your instructor. You should definitely consider using at least one sentence with *devoir.* No fewer than eight lines, no more than twelve.

_____
_____
_____
_____
_____
_____
_____
_____
_____
_____
_____
_____

Chapitre Quatorze

A. *Cassette.* You probably do not need this English version of the "dialogue" by this time in your study of French, but we won't break with the tradition we've established. Just read this version quickly, then listen to the recording of the postcard message, a number of times.

(at the top of the card):

Mr. D: How are things? All is well here. Would you do me a favor and read this note to the students in the Intensive French course? Thanks a lot.

(next is the printed text of the postcard, describing the photo):

> *N4755 - Biarritz - 64*
> *The fishing port, Sainte-Eugénie Church and the famous restaurant, "Albert"*

(finally, the short note for the students):

> I'm writing with the hope that this note will help encourage you. I was doing the exact same thing as you last year, and now, here I am in France. Thanks to the effectiveness of the program that you are taking, I can say that I'm one of the people in our group (there are 45 of us) who speaks French with the least difficulty. I'm very happy in France. Everywhere you look there's another photo to take. There are lots of people anxious to welcome foreigners. I hope you are doing well. Keep up the good work! . . . Yes, it's worth all the effort!

B. *Written.* Rewrite these short sentences, replacing the underlined expression by *y*. Remember that *y*, like the direct and indirect object pronouns, precedes the verb of which it is the complement.

1.   Je vais <u>à Paris</u>.

    _____.

2.   Elle pense <u>à cette question</u>.

    _____.

3.   Il est arrivé <u>à Strasbourg</u>.

    _____.

4.   Il met son revolver <u>sur la table</u>.

    _____.

C. *Written.* Answer the following questions, replacing the underlined expression by *y*, and supplying the rest of the answer yourself.

Model: Pourquoi allez-vous <u>en France</u>?
J'y vais parce que je veux apprendre le français.

1. Quand penses-tu <u>à tes examens</u>?

    _____.

2. Combien de fois sont-ils allés <u>à Paris</u>?

    _____.

3. Pendant combien de temps est-il resté <u>au Canada</u>?

    _____.

4. Pourquoi as-tu mis ton livre <u>sur le lit</u>?

    _____.

5. Quand est-ce que Marie est entrée <u>dans la cuisine</u>?

    _____.

D. *Cassette.* Answer the following questions, using *y* in your response.

Model: (You hear): Tu vas à Paris?
(You respond): **Oui, j'y vais.**

E. *Written.* Fill in the blank with the form of *suivre* that the context requires. Remember, as always, that the *futur proche* is normally a correct form to use to indicate future time.

(Michèle is telling a friend about the courses she and her brothers take..)

Le semestre passé, j' _____ un cours de chimie. C'était très intéressant, mais très difficile. Mes frères ont décidé de faire autre chose; ils _____ un cours de biologie. Ils ont dit que le prof était bien sympa, mais ils n'ont rien appris! Ce semestre je ne _____ que trois cours. À huit heures du matin je vais à la piscine pour un cours de natation. Mes deux frères _____ le même cours. Tout de suite après je dois me sécher les cheveux et courir au cours de maths. L'après-midi, j'ai un cours de philosophie. Le semestre prochain, je _____ quatre cours: maths, philosophie, littérature anglaise, et sociologie.

F. *Cassette.* Drill on the verb *suivre*.

G. *Written.* Rewrite each sentence, replacing the underlined words by *en.* Remember that *e n* , like *y,* and the direct and indirect object pronouns, precedes the verb of which it is the complement.

1. J'ai <u>du pain</u>.

   _____.

2. Nous n'avons pas <u>d'amis</u>.

   _____.

3. Il va acheter <u>du lait</u>.

   _____.

4. Il a vu <u>des avions</u>.

   _____.

5. Il n'a pas trouvé <u>de diamants</u>.

   _____.

H. *Written.* Answer the following questions, replacing the underlined expression by *en,* and supplying the remainder of the response yourself.

   Model: Où a-t-elle trouvé <u>de l'argent</u> ?
   Elle en a trouvé dans sa poche.

1. Pourquoi as-tu acheté <u>des oranges</u>?

   _____

2. Quand vas-tu chercher <u>des amis</u>?

   _____

3. Où trouve-t-on <u>des cochons</u>?

   _____

4. Combien <u>de frères</u> avez-vous?

   _____

5. Pourquoi posez-vous <u>des questions</u>?

   _____

I. *Cassette.* Drill on subjunctive forms, mainly of irregular verbs. We'll give a set of three models (listed below), which you are to repeat. Then we'll give new, short completions for each sentence, with the verb in the infinitive. Replace the underlined part of the model with the correct <u>subjunctive</u> form of the expression given as a cue.

1. Je veux qu'elle <u>fasse le dîner</u>.
2. Il faut que tu <u>partes tout de suite</u>.
3. Il vaut mieux que vous <u>m'écoutiez</u>.

J. *Written.* Answer the following questions, using your own words. Use the subjunctive if it is required.

1. Voulez-vous que je vous donne une bonne note?

   _____

2. Voulez-vous prendre le petit déjeuner dans la chambre?

   _____

3. Pourquoi veux-tu aller à ce restaurant?

   _____

4. Faut-il absolument que nous partions demain?

   _____

K. *Cassette. Dictée.*

1. _____.
2. _____
3. _____.
4. _____
5. _____.
6. _____,
7. _____.
8. _____,
9. _____
10. _____, _____ . . .

L. *Written.* You have expanded your horizons in French. To prove it, to yourself and to your instructor, return to one of the compositions you wrote earlier in the course (usually the final exercise in your workbook), read it quickly, then put it aside and rewrite it completely, trying to make it more interesting by using a greater variety of words and constructions. Make additional comments that involve talking about the past or the future, or that involve your stating your opinion about some aspect of what you said earlier.

_____

_____

_____

_____

_____

_____

_____

_____

_____

_____

_____

_____

_____

_____

Chapitre Quinze

A. *Cassette. Dialogue.* We provide below an English version of the dialogue in the Textbook. Please do not attempt to match words and lines: as always, our purpose is to give you a complete idea of what the dialogue is about, but not to provide a word-for-word translation. After you have read the version below, listen to the recording several times. If you wish to repeat, you may do so, but we do not leave pauses for repetition.

Charles Brown is majoring in French. He's happy with his major: he likes his courses, he loves the French language and its literature, and he has had the chance to study in France for one year. However, he's a bit anxious as a result of questions that his friends and his parents keep asking. He decides to go see his French professor and advisor. He knocks on the door . . .

Professor: Come in. Oh, hello Charles, how are you?

Charles: Fine, thanks. Do you have a minute?

Professor: Sure. What's on your mind?

Charles: Well, it's about French, but not about my courses. My friends and my family keep asking me: "What good is French going to do you?" Since I can't seem to find an answer myself, I thought I'd ask you for a good answer.

Professor: Hmm. Right....That's a good question. (Silence.) By learning a foreign language, you...mature...(Silence.) you become more cultured..you begin to understand the world a little better. . .

The phone rings. Relieved, the professor, after excusing himself, replies.

Professor: Hello? Babette? It's a pleasure to hear from you. You just got a job with SORTEC? Well, congratulations. It's an excellent ad agency. What's that? Because you know how to speak French they already gave you a raise and advancement? That's great; I'm really happy for you. Listen, you've called at just the right moment. I have a student in the office who is worried and would like to know if there are some good reasons to study French. Could you talk to him about your job? That's very good of you, thanks. . . Charles, here's a good answer.

And the professor passes the phone to Charles.

B. *Written.* Very simple, but very important, fill-in exercise. Rewrite each sentence we start, completing it with an appropriate time period, using *il y a* as in the model.

Model: J'ai acheté ma maison...
J'ai acheté ma maison il y a cinq ans.

1. Mes parents se sont mariés...

   _____.

2. On a fait exploser la première bombe atomique...

   _____.

3. Les cours ont commencé...

   _____.

4. Je suis arrivé(e) chez moi...

   _____.

5. J'ai conduit pour la première fois...

   _____.

6. Notre professeur est allé(e) en France...

   _____.

C. *Cassette.* Answer the following questions, using *il y a* and the period of time given as a cue.

Model: (we say:) Quand as-tu acheté cette maison?
(then we give a cue:) / cinq ans /
(YOU SAY:) **Je l'ai achetée il y a cinq ans.**

D. *Written.* Complete each of the following sentences with a (in most cases, <u>the</u>) form of the verb *recevoir* that fits the context.

1. Je _____ une lettre de mon fils toutes les semaines.

2. Autrefois, nous ne _____ des nouvelles de l'oncle Jim que quand il avait besoin d'argent, mais maintenant il nous écrit ou il nous téléphone très souvent.

3. Mes parents _____ des amis tous les samedis: ils ont presqu'un "salon" comme au dix-septième siècle.

4. Quand est-ce que tu _____ cette lettre? Hier?

5. J'espère que je _____ une réponse à cette lettre la semaine prochaine.

6. Le président _____ l'ambassadeur de l'Angleterre cet après-midi à trois heures, dans la salle ovale.

E. *Cassette.* Drill on the verb *recevoir.*

F. *Written.* Answer the following questions, using the expressions provided in parentheses. Be sure to write out your answer completely. This may seem easy, but it's important to work through each construction.

1. Quand est-elle née?

   a. (il y a 22 ans)

   _____.

   b. (en 1967)

   _____.

   c. (quand ses parents étaient en France)

   _____.

2. Quand as-tu reçu cette lettre?

   a. (il y a trois jours)

   _____.

   b. (mardi)

   _____.

   c. (quand j'ai reçu aussi la lettre de Louise)

   _____.

3. Quand est-ce que les étudiants ont fini l'examen?

   a. (il y a cinq minutes)

   _____.

   b. (à dix heures précises)

   _____.

   c. (quand le professeur a dit: "C'est l'heure!")

   _____.

G. *Written.* Now answer these "since when/how long" questions with *depuis* and a time expression, with the verb in the <u>present</u> tense. The condition or action started in the past, but <u>is still going on</u> .

   Model: Depuis quand travaille-t-elle dans cette boutique?
   Elle travaille dans cette boutique depuis quatre mois, c'est tout.

1. Depuis quand étudiez-vous le français?
   _____.

2. Depuis quand est-ce qu'il y a un métro à Paris?
   _____.

3. Depuis quand est-ce que le Canada est bilingue officiellement?
   _____.

4. Depuis quand fais-tu cet exercice?
   _____.

5. Depuis quand savez-vous nager?
   _____.

H. *Written.* Complete the following sentences with an appropriate form of one of the following verbs: *conduire, produire,* or *séduire.*

1. Depuis quand _____ -vous? (Attention!)
2. On dit que ce prof _____ une de ses étudiantes.
3. Les agriculteurs en France _____ beaucoup de blé.
4. a. -Vous, vous _____ une Cadillac, tandis que mois, je
      _____ une vieille Ford.
   b. -Oui, mais quand j'étais aussi jeune que vous, je _____ une
   ancienne Studebaker!

I. *Cassette.* Verb drill: *conduire, produire, séduire.*

Nom _____ **Cours** _____ **Section** _____

J. *Written.* Fill in the blank with the proper form of the verb given in parentheses.

1. (ÉCRIRE) Il est temps que nous _____ à Paul.
2. (FAIRE) Je suis content qu'ils _____ leurs devoirs.
3. (PRENDRE) Il est possible qu'elle _____ cette décision.
4. (FINIR) Il est logique qu'elle _____ avant nous.
5. (VENIR) Nous sommes désolés que tu ne _____ pas ce soir.
6. (ETRE) Elle est heureuse que nous _____ venus.
7. (AVOIR) Il est possible qu'ils _____ raison.
8. (DIRE) Je suis fâchée que tu _____ cela, chéri.

K. *Cassette.* We're going to give two cue-phrases in a row. You repeat the second one as the beginning of your response, then add the first one, making any necessary changes.

Model: (we say:) / elle part /
(then we say:) / je suis content /
(YOU RESPOND:) **Je suis content qu'elle parte.**

L. *Cassette. Dictée.* Usual system.

1. Client: _____
2. _____ .
3. _____ ?
4. Vendeur: _____
5. _____ .
6. Client: _____ , _____ .
7. Vendeur: _____
8. _____ .
9. Client: _____ .
10. _____ .

M.   *Cassette.*   Word and sound discrimination.

/ attend - entend - un temps /   _____

/ vend - vendent - vendons /   _____

/ perd - perdent - perdez /   _____

/ le - la - les /   _____

/ bout - but - bu /   _____

N.   *Written.*   Composition.
Write a single, cohesive paragraph, describing or commenting on something that you started doing some time ago and still do today (or an attitude or opinion that you had in the past and have not lost or changed).   You must start with (or end with) a sentence that contains the "present idiomatic" construction, as in the model (underlined).   Aside from that restriction, you are free to discuss past situations or current ones, or future ones.

Model: J'adore l'université depuis six mois.   C'est vrai que quand je suis venue ici il y a deux ans, je n'étais pas contente.   La première année était pénible: je ne connaissais personne, et je détestais mes cours et mes profs.   Mais le semestre passé, j'ai commencé à étudier le français.   Alors tout a changé.   J'ai des amis maintenant.   Je participe au "cercle français".   L'été prochain, je vais aller en France.   Que je suis heureuse!

(Suggestions, but you are not limited to these! --You love pizza now, but you used to like only hamburgers; you swim every day; you read the newspaper; you study on weekends instead of going out.   NB: these are ideas for topics.   DO NOT try to translate them: choose words you know.)

_____

_____

_____

_____

_____

_____

_____

_____

_____

_____

_____

_____

_____

_____

_____

_____

Chapitre Seize

A. *Cassette.* Read the following English version of the dialogues that are in your text, then listen to the taped version a number of times. As usual, you may--if you wish--stop the tape at various intervals and repeat sections of the dialogue, but we are mainly interested in your developing listening comprehension: listen <u>without</u> looking at either version of the text. We also recommend that you try repeating as you listen to the tape (simultaneously).

Dialogue 1.

A crowd of people gather around the paintings of the artist Toto, who is the star today. But where is the artist? Did he perhaps skip out to go to the Faucette movie house?

A man who has been sipping champagne for more than an hour and a rather large lady who's filling herself with snacks find themselves together in front of a canvas entitled: "Impression--sunset."

Mme de Bouffix: Oh, my dear sir, the power that this painting has on my soul cannot be expressed! My heart is touched and I laugh and I cry, so strongly does this painting express your genius. I congratulate you on its success. As I look into your eyes, I see there the same fire that burns in the colors of your canvases. Please permit a humble admirer who thought that modern art had nothing further to reveal to shake your hand with warmth and to express to you all of her admiration.

M. de Pinard: Dear lady, you flatter me and honor me, but . . . I am not the artist. I must unfortunately undeceive you. I've come here only to drink some champagne . . . free.

Mme de Bouffis: Sir, you shock me and your attitude is inexcusable--trying to make me believe you were the artist. I <u>only</u> converse with cultured people, not with the common herd. But where is Toto, the artist?

Dialogue 2.

Cultural activities on the weekend. A discussion among friends.

Valérie: Last night, I went to a private showing by a painter. FAN--TAS--TIQUE! The artist totally knows how to express an astonishing melancholy that was at times even esoteric! I'm still all goose bumps, so thoroughly was I impressed by those canvases.

Gérard: As for me, on the other hand, I went to the theater: a play by Pinget: I can describe the experience in one word - SUBLIME!!!!

Constance: Well, modern art is not bad, but I really prefer classical. Is there anything comparable to a symphony of Beethoven, a ballet by the great Balanchine, a Verdi opera? Don't you agree, Albert?

Albert: Um. Errr. Yes, you're right, all of you.

Gérard: And what cultural activity do you participate in passionately each weekend?

Valérie, Constance and Gérard are silent and watch Albert, waiting anxiously for an answer.

Albert: Er... Uh... (He clears his throat.) As for me, I spend my weekends, er, watching stupid shows on TV.

B. *Written.* Fill in the blanks in the following sentences with the correct form of the interrogative pronoun. Pay attention to context to see if it concerns a <u>person</u> or a <u>thing</u>. (See the *Reference Grammar*, 1.6.1)

1. _____ est assis sur le trône? Je suis sur que ce n'est pas le roi.
2. _____ est dans votre valise, monsieur?
3. Chez _____ allons-nous dîner ce soir?
4. -- _____ faites-vous le weekend? -Absolument rien.
5. À _____ est-ce que vous avez révélé mon secret?
6. _____ est-ce que vous avez offert à Marie pour son anniversaire?
7. _____ est-ce que Charles a épousé?

C. *Cassette.* These are the *Questions et réponses-A et -B* exercises from your text, really dialogues. Please repeat with your text closed.

D. *Written.* Fill in the blanks in the following sentences with the correct form of the interrogative adjective. Remember that the interrogative adjective can function either as a determiner (directly in front of the noun it modifies) or as a predicate adjective (on the other side of the verb *être*) and that it agrees in gender and number with the noun that it modifies. DO NOT USE the interrogative pronoun in this exercise, even when it might be acceptable.

1. --Si on allait au cinéma? -Je veux bien. _____ film veux-tu voir?
2. -- _____ animaux sont les plus féroces? -Les hommes.
3. _____ est votre profession?
4. --À _____ étage habitent-ils? -Au cinquième, la porte à droite.
5. _____ sont ces femmes?
6. Dans _____ boutique as-tu trouvé cette jupe? C'est chic.

E. *Written.* Complete the following sentences with the appropriate form of the verb *croire*.

1. Tu mens toujours. Je ne te _____ plus.
2. _____ -vous que le prof travaille autant que nous?
3. Autrefois, elle _____ à ce système politique.
4. Monique! Ne fais pas cela! On _____ que tu es folle!
5. Est-ce que les étudiants _____ vraiment que nous n'allons pas avoir de cours demain?

F. *Cassette.* Drill on the verb *croire*. Usual pattern.

G. *Written.* Write a question that would naturally elicit the response given, using any words given in parentheses and using an interrogative pronoun (QUI-type) or an interrogative adjective. The **bold** segment indicates what the question asked about. There is often more than one possibility, but take the time to try to produce the most appropriate question. THINK about what each response means, but do not translate.

Model: (devant la bibliothèque)
Qui attendiez-vous devant la bibliothèque? (or use tu)
    J'attendais **Jean-Philippe.**

1. (notre professeur / à sa femme)

_____

    Il lui a offert **un collier d'émeraudes.**

2. (l'agent de police)

_____

    Cette réponse l'a surpris.

3. _____

    Il n'y a **rien** sur la table.

4. _____

    Nous parlons du film **que nous avons vu hier soir.**

5. (aller au grand bal avec lui)

_____

    Il va inviter **Marie-Antoinette.**

6. (voiture)

_____

Je préfère **la** voiture **de sport italienne.**

H. *Written.* This is basically a study sheet for subjunctive verb forms. All of the blanks require a subjunctive form because that verb is in a subordinate clause introduced by one of the conjunctions that always take the subjunctive. Give the proper form of the appropriate verb from the pool we have provided. Do not use any verb more than once.

/ _ aller   _ dire   _ être   _ avoir   _ comprendre   _ finir /

1. Je t'ai di cela afin que tu _____ mes réactions.
2. Il faut conduire plus vite afin que nous _____ à l'heure.
3. Ils ne parlent pas français, bien qu'ils _____ à Paris très souvent.
4. Moi, je ne vais pas attendre jusqu'à ce qu'il _____ ce long discours.
5. Quoi que tu _____ , je ne peux pas te croire.
6. C'est scandaleux! Bien qu'il _____ toujours tort, on le croit.

I. *Written.* Fill in the blank with the preposition/particle that goes with the main verb before a complementary infinitive: either *à* or *de.* If the verb takes no preposition/particle before the infinitive, write in an x.

1. Prof: --Nous allons _____ commencer maintenant.

2. Jean: --Moi, je ne veux pas _____ faire cet exercice.

3. Prof: --Très bien. M. le sergent, demandez à cet étudiant _____ partir... gentiment, bien entendu.

4. Jean: --Oh! je vous demande pardon, madame. Mais je vous assure que j'ai essayé _____ faire cet exercice chez moi et c'était impossible.

5. Prof: --Très bien, je vous permets _____ rester dans la salle, mais si vous continuez _____ m'interrompre, c'est fini.

J. *Cassette.* Word and sound discrimination. Write the word that you hear.

1. / fille - fils - fil /   _____

2. / gare - guerre - car /   _____

3. / sort - sortent - sortait /   _____

4. / en - on - au /   _____

5. / vu - vois - vous /   _____

6. / bon - bonne - beau /   _____

K. *Dictée.* Write during the second reading. We'll give line numbers.

1. _____

2. _____

3. _____.

4. _____?

5. _____?

6. _____

7. _____ ,

8. _____

9. _____ , _____ Attila,

10. _____.

L. *Cassette.* Write a brief and concise plot summary of a film you have seen recently. We'd prefer that it be a French film, but realize that it may not be a reasonable request. Remember, as always, to keep it simple. On the other hand, you should not now be limiting yourself to the verbs *être*, *avoir* and *aller:* use the vocabulary lists in the *intégration* units to get ideas. (Procedure: choose the film, sketch an outline of the plot, scan the word lists, write a little, put it aside, think some more about a simple statement of the facts, return to writing. Don't try to do it all in one sitting.

Use only the space provided. No more. Start with: *Dans* (name of film) *il s'agit de...*

_____
_____
_____
_____
_____
_____
_____
_____
_____
_____
_____
_____
_____
_____
_____
_____
_____
_____
_____
_____
_____
_____

Chapitre Dix-Sept

A. *Cassette.* Read the following English version of the dialogue in the text first, then listen, following the usual pattern.

Narrator:	*Nathalie and Marie-France are strolling along the "quais" of the Seine River in Paris. Nathalie feels like doing something, but not Marie-France.*
Nathalie:	Don't you feel like going to the theatre?
Marie-France:	What would you like to see?
Nathalie:	A tragedy by Racine, *Phèdre.* It's gotten good write-ups on the staging and on the acting.
Marie-France:	I don't like tragedies. They're always so pessimistic. How about going to eat at the *Tour d'argent?*
Nathalie:-	You're crazy! It's too expensive and besides it's not cultural. On the other hand, going to see a tragedy is a significant cultural experience.
Marie-France:	Maybe for you, but for me it's too boring. I'd rather eat in a good restaurant. Let's have something; I'm very hungry.
Nathalie:	Oh, you... You're always hungry. Well, okay, we have the time.
Narrator:	*They enter a restaurant and Marie-France chooses a table in the back. They come out an hour later.*
Nathalie:	Oh, damn! Look at the time! We're going to be late for the play. Taxi! Taxi!
Marie-France:	(with a sly smile) -It's really a shame.

B. *Cassette.* Verb review drill. There will be one of these in every chapter from now on. We'll follow the usual verb drill pattern, except that each new set (four altogether) will involve a different verb--possibly in a different tense, although we'll emphasize the present tense forms. In this review, we'll work with *avoir, faire, aller,* and *dire.*

C. *Written.* What we give in quotes is what someone said at some moment in the past. Complete the sentence (started for you in parentheses) that <u>reports</u> that utterance, putting the verb in the appropriate tense: *l'imparfait* if the original was in *le présent*; le conditionnel simple if the original was in *le futur.* Pay attention to who is reporting the statement, so as to keep your pronoun use natural and correct.

> **Model:** **a.** "Je suis malade." (Vous avez dit que...)
> **Vous avez dit que vous étiez malade.**
> **b.** "Je partirai demain." (Marie a dit que...)
> **Marie a dit qu'elle partirait demain/aujourd'hui.**

1. "Je leur en parlerai ce soir." (Tu as dit que...)

   _____

2. "Ma femme est fatiguée." (Jean-Pierre a dit que...)

   _____

3. "Nous ferons ces exercices la semaine prochaine." (Elle a dit que...)

   _____

4. "Vous aurez le temps d'écrire cet examen avec soin." (Vous avez dit que...)

   _____

5. "Cela m'est égal." (Tu as dit que...)

   _____

6. "Tu seras très contente." (Tu m'as dit que...)

   _____

7. "Marie viendra à la fête." (Paul nous a assuré que...)

   _____

8. "Si tu m'aides, je te donnerai 5.000 francs." (Tu m'as dit que...)

   _____

D. *Cassette.* Becoming familiar with the various uses of *TOUT.* Answer the following questions, always using a form of *TOUT* in your response. Sometimes it will be used in the question, sometimes not. There will often be more than one way to insert a use of *TOUT,* but we'll give only one "correct" response on the tape. As usual, give your response, then listen to (but do not repeat) the response we suggest.

> **Model:** **a.** Avez-vous tout préparé?
> **Oui, j'ai tout préparé.**
> **b.** Est-ce que les étudiants sont venus?
> **Oui, ils sont tous venus.**

E. *Written.* Fill in the proper form of *TOUT*, pronoun, adjective or adverb, in the following sentences.

1. Je réponds de la qualité de _____ les voitures dans ce salon.
2. Ces profs! Ils sont _____ trop sévères.
3. Bien, je te l'ai expliqué encore une fois. _____ est clair?
4. J'ai passé _____ la matinée à la bibliothèque.
5. On a détruit _____ les bâtiments.
6. Ces ratons ont mangé _____ le pain qui était sur la table!
7. Nous sommes _____ trop paresseux.
8. _____ est pour le mieux dans le meilleur des mondes.

F. *Written.* Complete the following sentences using the verbs *mourir, boire,* or *naître.* Any of them may be used more than once. Pay careful attention to the context in order to give the right verb form.

1. a. Victor Hugo _____ en 1802, à Besançon.

   b. Il _____ en 1885.

2. a. Hier soir, je _____ de soif.

   b. Donc, j' _____ cinq bouteilles de bière.

   c. Ce matin, mon médecin m'a dit que je _____ dans quelques mois si je continuais à _____ comme ça.

G. *Cassette.* Verb drill: *mourir.*

H. *Cassettte.* Word and sound discrimination.

1. / douzième - deuxième / _____
2. / viens - venons - venait / _____
3. / tenions - tenons - tenez / _____
4. / venu - voulu - vu / _____

I. *Cassette.* Aural comprehension. Listen to the mini-dialogues. In each case, indicate if the response is appropriate and logical by writing *oui* if it is, *non* if it isn't.

1. _____ 2. _____ 3. _____ 4. _____ 5. _____

J. *Cassette. Dictée.*

1. Le patron: _____ , _____ .

2. _____ ?

3. L'employé: _____ , _____ ?

4. _____

5. _____

6. _____ .

7. Le patron: _____ !

8. _____ ,

9. _____

10. L'employé: _____ .

K. *Written.* Write a short composition in response to the question we will pose, using principally the conditional tense (it will be the most natural tense to use--for most sentences--if you follow the instructions).

Question: Que feriez-vous si vous étiez obligé de passer six mois dans une maison à la campagne sans parler à personne? (On apporterait des provisions tous les lundis et vous auriez tous les appareils: TV, radio, réfrigérateur, etc.)

Si on m'obligeait de passer six mois tout(e) seul(e) dans cette maison, je... _____

_____

_____

_____

_____

_____

_____

_____

_____

_____

_____

_____

_____

_____

_____

_____

Chapitre Dix-Huit

A. *Cassette.* You're going to hear two additional excerpts from the *Paris Pas Cher* guidebook that provided the lecture passages of *Chapitre Dix* in the textbook.

    The first one is about a stationery store, something like a university bookstore, and there are just a few new words. Some are cognates. You'll hear "*papeterie*" which means 'stationery store' and you'll hear "*idem*," the Latin word, which is used fairly often in French, meaning 'the same' or--colloquially--'ditto'.

    The second one is worth trying to understand if you like the most recent popular music and have some cash when you go to Paris. It's about a DJ who "caters" his music to parties in Paris. You'll note they use the same word for "*disc-jockey*." Catch also that he provides special lighting effects *(éclairages spéciaux)* and even "*la fumée (inodore et sans danger)*." They tell you when you can reach him by phone, even on Sundays.

B. *Cassette.* Just repeat the sentences given in this exercise. All include the use of either *jouer à* or *jouer de* or both.

C. *Written.* Rewrite completely each of the following sentences, replacing the active *on*-construction with a passive construction. In general, the tense of the verb that goes with *on* will be the tense of the <u>auxiliary</u> in the passive construction.

Model: On plantera ces arbres demain.
        Ces arbres seront plantés demain.

1. On fabrique ces téléviseurs à l'étranger.

    _____

2. On a distribué ces pamphlets partout.

    _____

3. On construira un pont à cet endroit.

    _____

4. On applaudirait une telle décision.

    _____

5. Il faut qu'*on répète cette phrase plusieurs fois*.

    (It is the italicized clause that should be made passive.)

    _____

D. *Written.* As in *C*, we want you to rewrite, using a passive construction, but you'll notice that all the cue-sentences have their verbs in the *passé simple.* The intention is to give you some more practice recognizing the past definite forms and also to help you become familiar with one of the more common passive types: the past definite of the verb *être* + past participle. Since the only objects in our cue sentences will be in the 3rd person, all you'll have to produce (since the direct objects become the grammatical subjects of the passive sentences) are *fut* (3rd singular) and *furent* (3rd plural).

Model: Napoléon conquit l'Allemagne.
L'Allemagne fut conquise par Napoléon.

1. Hannibal traversa les Alpes.

   _____

2. Les explorateurs français ouvrirent ce passage.

   _____

3. Edison inventa la lampe électrique.

   _____

4. Gorbachev fit ce premier pas.

   _____

E. *Cassette.* Verb drill. Since *plaire* has only one very common construction type, we'll just include it with the three verbs we want to review in this chapter: *être, lire,* and *partir.*

F. *Written.* Controlled review of the *passé composé.* In set (1), you have only *"être"* verbs; in set (2), *"avoir"* verbs; in set (3), reflexive verbs. Then in the longer set, (4), we mix them. Write in the correct form of the verb given in parentheses, in the *passé composé.*

1. a. (aller)   Nous _____ au théâtre hier soir.

   b. (monter)   Elle _____ au cinquième étage.

   c. (rester)   Ils _____ chez lui toute la matinée.

2. a. (frapper)   J' _____ mon petit frère.

   b. (boire)   Ils _____ tout le vin.

   c. (marcher)   Elle _____ pendant des heures.

3. a. (se laver)   Elle _____ les mains.

   b. (se lever)   Je _____ à six heures ce matin.

   c. (se voir)   Nous _____ hier au concert.

4. a. (voyager)   Nous _____ en Espagne l'été dernier.

   b. (passer)   Moi, j' _____ tout l'été à New York.

   c. (venir)   Marie _____ me voir ce matin.

   d. (s'amuser) On _____ à regarder de vieux films en noir et blanc.

   e. (pleuvoir) Est-ce qu'il _____ hier à Bordeaux?

   f. (mourir)   Hitler _____ dans un incendie. Enfin, c'est ce qu'on dit.

   g. (mettre)   Tu _____ trop de livres sur cette étagère.

   h. (se rencontrer) Ils _____ dans le parc.

G. *Written.*   Fill in the blanks with the proper form of the appropriate verb from the "pool," including--as necessary--a preposition/particle to connect it to the complementary infinitive. See the *Reference Grammar*, 12.1, and/or use your dictionary to check whether or not the verb takes a particle or preposition with a complementary infinitive. DO NOT USE ANY VERB MORE THAN ONCE, that is, from each group of five.

/ __ ne pas réussir   __ offrir   __ aller   __ espérer   __ refuser   __ continuer /

1. Le jeune homme _____ perdre tout son argent.

2. Les joueurs _____ jouer malgré tout ce qu'ils perdent.

3. Ils _____ regagner tout "la prochaine fois".

4. Leurs amis _____ les encourager de cesser de jouer.

5. En fin de compte, ils _____ écouter les conseils de leurs amis.

/ __ vouloir   __ dire   __ apprendre   __ décider   __ inviter
                __ aller   __ essayer /

6. Marie parlait avec son agent de voyage hier. Enfin, elle _____ aller à Paris pendant les vacances de Pâques.

7. Elle _____ voir le spectacle qu'on _____ présenter sur le parvis de la Cathédrale de Notre-Dame.

8. On lui _____ ne pas manquer cette occasion. C'est *La Passion* d'Arnoul Gréban et on ne la présente que rarement.

9. En effet, elle _____ y assister la dernière fois, en 1953, mais elle n'a pas pu.

10. Cette fois-ci, une très bonne amie l' _____ l'accompagner, et elle a réservé deux places excellentes.

H. *Cassette.* Write *oui* if the response in the mini-dialogue is logical and appropriate; write *non* if it is not.

1. _____   2. _____   3. _____   4. _____

I. *Cassette.* Word and sound discrimination. Write the word that you hear.

1. / lavé - laver - lavez /   _____
2. / lisais - lisions - lisez /   _____
3. / dorment - dormait - dormez - dormaient /   _____
4. / se - sa - ses /   _____
5. / couramment - constamment - continuellement /   _____

J. *Cassette. Dictée.*

1. _____
2. _____*Blanche-Neige.*_____
3. _____
4. _____
5. _____.
6. _____,
7. _____.
8. _____
9. _____.
10. _____,_____
11. _____ ... _____

Chapitre Dix-Neuf

A. *Cassette.* The following "translation" (it is, as usual, not a close translation, but rather an English equivalent) of the dialogue on the tape/cassette program for this chapter is the only text you'll have for this section. What is on the cassette is a dialogue, not a recording of the set of short letters that you have in the text.

Narrator:	*Professor Grosdidier invites his students to join him for some refreshment at the "Académie", but they don't understand right away.*
Professor:	Anybody want to go to the *Académie* with me?
Sylvie:	No, thanks, I'd rather stay here.
Professor:	But, . . . you get a really wide choice there.
Sylvie:	Maybe so, but in my opinion we already have enough to do without going to any academy.
Yves:	Oh, come on, Sylvie. If the prof wants to show us something new we ought to go along. Where is this academy, Professor Grosdidier?
Professor:	Not far. You can get there on foot: go up the Boul' Mich' to the Boulevard Port-Royal, turn to the left and it's on your left.
Yves:	Hmm. I don't follow you. I don't know of any academy near there.
Professor:	Of course not. I'm not talking about a school. I'm talking about the *"Académie de la Bière."*
Jean-Luc:	OK, I know what you're talking about. Let's go, especially if the prof's paying.
Yves:	Sure, I know what the *Académie* is. I wouldn't mind having a *sérieux* of Kronenbourg.
Professor:	Everyone's coming then? Finish up these exercises and we'll take off.
Sylvie:	I don't like beer. I'm staying here.

B. *Cassette.* Repeat the following phrases, paying careful attention to the relative clauses that further idenitfy the person or thing referred to.

C. *Written.* Complete each sentence by writing in the proper form of the verb *mettre.* Be sure to consider the entire context.

1. -- Tu veux faire une promenade?

    -- Oui, mais il fait un peu frais. Attends. Je vais _____ un pull.

2. -- Qui _____ la table?

    -- Moi. Je l'ai fait à midi. Pourquoi?

    -- Parce qu'il n'y a pas de fourchettes!

3. L'année passée, quand on insistait sur l'ancienne limite de vitesse, je _____

    six heures pour aller à St. Louis.

4. Ils _____ toujours leurs pantoufles avant d'entrer dans le salon.

D. *Cassette.* Verb drill on *mettre.*

E. *Written.* Fill in the blanks with the proper form of the relative pronoun (*qui,* if it is the subject of the verb in the relative clause; *que,* if it is the object: it makes no difference what the antecedent is).

1. Voilà le garçon _____ j'ai vu dans le bureau du doyen.

2. Le monsieur _____ me parlait dans le couloir est un acteur célèbre.

3. La robe _____ elle portait hier soir était trop décolletée.

4. Combien as-tu payé la voiture _____ tu viens d'acheter?

5. C'est vous _____ avez mis les disques dans le frigo?

6. Où sont les gants _____ je vous ai prêtés hier?

7. Tous les étudiants _____ veulent travailler sérieusement peuvent réussir dans ce cours.

8. Où est le sac _____ était sur cette table quand je suis entré?

F. *Written.* Answer each of the following questions using a relative clause in your response, as in the model. The point is to give a fairly detailed reply, supplying sufficient information to be helpful and informative.

Model: Qui est ce monsieur?
C'est l'agent de police qui m'a aidé hier quand on m'a attaqué dans le parc.

1. Qui est cette dame?

   _____

2. Ce livre est à vous?

   _____

3. De quel film parlez-vous?

   _____

4. Quel cheval est-ce?

   _____

5. À quel étudiant a-t-on donné le prix?

   _____

6. Dans quelle assiette dois-je mettre le fromage?

   _____

G. *Written.* Answer the following questions using the demonstrative pronoun. Use all three of the possible completion forms, each one at least twice.

Model: Laquelle de ces photos préfères-tu?
Je préfère celle que Jean a prise.

1. Lesquelles de ces pâtisseries va-t-on acheter?

   _____

2. Laquelle des fenêtres était fermée?

   _____

3. Lequel de vos fils est devenu avocat?

   _____

4. Lequel de vos cours est le plus facile?

   _____

5. Lesquels de ses clients sont sympathiques?

   _____

6. Laquelle des salles est la plus petite?

   _____

7. Lequel de ces plats a le meilleur goût?

   _____

8. Lesquels de ces souvenirs allez-vous garder pour toujours?

   _____

H. *Written.* Fill in the blanks in the following sentences with the correct form of the interrogative pronoun *lequel* (LQL). You must read the entire sentence or mini-dialogue with care to see if the question deals with one (thus a singular form required) or more (plural) persons or objects.

1. -- _____ de ces pommes veux-tu?

   -- Celle que tu as déjà goûtée.

2. _____ de ces fleurs est une rose?

3. _____ de vos étudiants sont déjà allés en France?

4. -- Tu sais, un de nos collègues vient de recevoir le Prix Nobel en littérature.

   -- Tiens, _____ . . . ou devrais-je dire _____?

   -- Tu as deviné! Oui, c'est Madame Planchon.

5. _____ de ces sculptures sont à vendre?

I. *Written.* Review of *l'imparfait,* forms. Fill in the blank with the correct form of the verb, in the imperfect tense.

1. (boire)   À cette époque, je _____ jour et nuit.

2. (avoir)   Ils _____ tort, mais ils ne voulaient pas l'avouer.

3. (obéir)   Quand j'étais enfant, j' _____ toujours à mes parents.

4. (croire)   Tu le _____?

5. (perdre)   Mon grand-père _____ ses lunettes deux ou trois fois par jour.

6. (lire)   Autrefois, nous ne _____ que des romans policiers.

J. *Cassette.* Verb drill review, including *savoir, connaître, prendre,* and *vouloir.*

K. *Cassette.* Word/sound discrimination. Write the word(s) that you hear.

1. / dit - dites - dix /   _____

2. / j'ai - chez - je /   _____

3. / moins - mois - mon /   _____

4. / faim - femme - fin /   _____

5. / et - ai - êtes /   _____

L. *Cassette. Dictée.* Usual pattern.

Chez le médecin, dans la salle d'attente.

1. -- _____ .
2. _____ .
3. -- _____ , _____ ,
4. _____ .
5. -- _____ .
6. _____ .
7. -- _____ , _____ ,
8. _____ .
9. -- _____ .
10. -- _____ . _____ !

M. *Written.* Composition. Following is a list of things you might want to do in the future. Choose any three and write a short composition (use only the space provided) that ties them together.

__ avoir un métier intéressant,   __ faire le tour du monde,   __ obtenir son diplôme,

__ apprendre à parler une autre langue étrangère,   __ habiter à la campagne,

__ acheter une maison,   __ être heureux,   __ se marier et avoir des enfants.

(Check the three that you have used.)

_____
_____
_____
_____
_____
_____
_____
_____
_____
_____
_____
_____
_____
_____
_____
_____
_____
_____
_____
_____
_____
_____
_____
_____
_____
_____
_____

Chapitre Vingt

A. *Cassette.* As always, we ask you to read this English version of the dialogue in your textbook rapidly, just to be sure you know what it is about. Then listen to the recorded version frequently, at various times, preferably without looking at either text.

It's a beautiful sunny day, not a cloud in the sky. A family has just settled down on the beach. The children go off to play in the sand.

Mother: (to the father) There you are, my pet, you can stretch out in the lawn chair under the umbrella. I'll lie down here alongside you on the sand in the sun.

She checks on the children and suddenly cries out:

Monique, be careful, don't get too close to the water! Zoé, don't go over by that lady, stay here! Yves, don't touch the doggie!

Father: Damn! I left my newspaper and my sunglasses in the car.

Mother: Don't worry about it, sweetheart, I'll go get them, stay right there.

She goes off and returns a few minutes later.

There you are, honey.

Zoé begins to cry. The mother, angered, says:

Yves, give Zoé her toys back!

Yves is crying. The mother cries out:

Zoé, stop right now hitting your brother with your shovel. If you kids don't stop fighting, your father's going to get up and . . . .

Father: Oh, let them play, they have to let off steam once in a while.

. . . a little later

Mother: Come here, children, there's a cool breeze. I want you to slip on your T-shirts or you're going to catch cold.

Children: But, ma, it's too hot out.

Mother: Do as I say, don't complain.

Father: If only I could have a little peace!

B. *Written.* Practice with reflexive constructions. In the following sentences, complete the blanks, as appropriate, with a reflexive pronoun, an auxiliary, or the ending of the past participle.

1. Pardon. Je dois _____ dépêcher.

2. Pourquoi _____ sont-ils rencontr _____ à la bibliothèque?

3. Dis, Marie, tu t' _____ amus _____ au bal hier soir?

4. À quelle heure _____ lèves-tu d'habitude?

5. On _____ voit presque tous les dimanches depuis mon retour.

6. Elle s'est lav ____ les mains avant de préparer le dîner.

C. *Cassette.* Verb review drill: *pouvoir, sortir, écrire.*

D. *Written.* Fill in the blanks with the proper form of the relative pronoun. Note that this exercise includes relative pronouns functioning as the subject or object of the verb *(Chapitre 19)*, as well as the object of a preposition.

1. C'est le chirurgien _____ a sauvé la vie au général.

2. C'est le chat _____ a mangé la souris _____ a mangé le fromage _____ la fermière a fait.

3. Où est le revolver avec _____ il a assassiné le ministre?

4. Dans ce village il y a une église en face de[1] _____ on trouve une très jolie fontaine du Moyen Age.

5. La personne à _____ je pense est très jeune, est célèbre, et elle habite en France, à Nice.

6. Les questions _____ il nous a posées n'étaient pas très difficiles.

7. Le verre _____ était sur la table ne contenait pas de vin.

8. La rue dans _____ ce musée se trouve est difficile à trouver.

9. Le prof _____ va donner l'examen vient d'arriver.

10. Le pauvre homme _____ la police a arrêté était en effet la victime!

E. *Cassette.* Answer the following questions, paying careful attention to the tense of the question and to the proper formation of the reflexive construction. As usual, we'll give correct answers (there may be more than one possible in some cases--we'll just give one). Do not try to repeat the correct answers: rather, if you find you made a number or errors, repeat the entire exercise.

---

1. Yes, there is a *de* here, and we told you that *de* + relative prounoun becomes *dont*. However, this *de* is part of the three-word preposition *en face de* and therefor does not take on that special form. The same is true for any multi-word preposition that ends in *de*, such as *à cause de* or *à propos de*.

F. *Written.* Complete the blanks with the proper form of *faire*.

1. Je _____ mes devoirs tous les jours depuis le premier jour du semestre.

2. Quand je suis sorti ce matin, il _____ froid; maintenant il _____ très chaud.

3. Regarde ces enfants! Ils ne _____ jamais attention à leur père.

4. -- Tu _____ du ski?

5. -- Non, enfin oui: je _____ du ski nautique.

G. *Written.* Answer the following questions, all in the negative.

Model: Tu t'es amusé hier soir?
Non, je ne me suis pas amusé hier soir.

1. Se sont-ils vus pendant les vacances?
    _____

2. Est-ce que vous vous êtes dépêchés?
    _____

3. C'est vrai? Elle s'appelle Sylvie Bouton?
    _____

4. Est-ce que tu t'es levé(e) de bonne heure ce matin?
    _____

5. Nous nous sommes trompés, n'est-ce pas?
    _____

H. *Cassette.* Word and sound discrimination.

1. / aller - allés - allez /   _____

2. / attend - entend - attendent - entendent /   _____

3. / rentré - rentrer - rentrez /   _____

4. / la - l'as - le /   _____

5. / ses - ces - c'est /   _____

I. *Cassette. Dictée.*

1. -- _____ !

2. -- _____

3. _____ ,

4. _____

5. _____ .

6. _____ *Zénith.*

7. _____ .

8. -- _____ ! _____ .

J. *Written.* Composition, to be written on a separate piece of lined paper, size 8 1/2 X 11. Leave one inch margins (at least) left and right, and double-space. Use a pen (blue or black, not red or green). This composition will be corrected, then revised before a grade is given, but the quality of the first draft will affect your grade, so do your best from the start.

Write a well-organized composition of one to one and a half pages on any topic you choose. Keep within the vocabulary and constructions you know! (Use the *Intégration* lists first, then the text glossary: use a dictionary only if it is absolutely necessary for one or two key words.)

Chapitre Vingt et Un

A. *Cassette.* Listen to the dialogue that is on the cassette. We do not give you the text in written form at all, but will tell you that it's a conversation that takes place in a student snack-bar area at a French university, between a young man and a girl that he recognizes as a former acquaintance from his *lycée*. Some possibly unfamiliar words you will hear are: *la berlue* (*avoir la berlue* means "to be imagining things"); *déménagé* (*déménager* means "to move"); *malin* ("sly, mischievious"); *taquiner* ("to tease").

B. *Written.* Verb distinctions (meaning). From each pair of verbs in parentheses, select the one which properly completes the sentence and fill in the blank with the appropriate form of that verb.

1. (partir / quitter)   Nous devrions _____ la stade avant la fin du match.

2. (partir / sortir)   Est-ce que Philippe _____ pour Aix-en-Provence ce soir?

3. (quitter / sortir)   Les touristes qui _____ du Louvre trop tard ont découvert que les autocars ne les attendaient plus!

4. (partir / quitter)   Est-ce que tu _____ en vacances en décembre?

5. (sortir / quitter)   L'espion 007 _____ un stylo de sa poche et a fait exploser le paquet.

C. *Written.* Make one sentence out of each pair of sentences, joining them with *après, avant,* or *en.* Remember that you must change the verb form of the clause that you introduce with one of those connector expressions. We indicate which connector to use for the first three; after that you must choose one that is appropriate (and that will depend on which sentence you choose as the main clause).

Model: Je me suis habillée. Je me suis levée. (après)
Je me suis habillée après m'être levée.

1. J'ai dit bonjour. Je suis entré dans le bureau du prof. (après)

   _____

2. J'ai étudié pendant trois heures. Je me suis couché. (avant)

   _____

3. Je suis arrivée à l'heure. J'ai couru très vite. (en)

   _____

4. Elle se repose. Elle regarde la télévision.

   _____

5. Tu as décidé de partir. Tu m'as parlé de ce problème.

   _____

6. Ils devraient faire leurs devoirs. Ils viennent en classe.

   _____

7. Il a bu trop de bière. Il a eu mal à la tête.

   _____

8. Elle s'est cassé la jambe. Elle faisait du ski.

   _____

D. *Cassette.* You'll hear the speaker say he/she did something, using a time expression for which either *toute la journée, toute la matinée, toute l'année,* or *toute la soirée* is an equivalent expression. You respond, saying <u>to the person</u>, "Oh, you did X," substituting the proper equivalent expression for the one you hear.

Model: (You hear) J'ai étudié hier soir *de huit heures jusqu'à minuit.*
(You respond) **Ah! tu as étudié toute la soirée!**

NB: The answers we will provide are somewhat exaggerated. The important thing to listen for is the expression, *toute la soirée,* etc.

E. *Written.* Complete the blanks in the following sentences with an "indefinite" demonstrative adjective (*ce, cet, cette, ces*), or an indefinite pronoun (*ceci, cela, ça, ce*), or an indefinite quantifier (*quelques, plusieurs, chaque*). Read the whole sentence or extended context before answering.

1. Il y avait _____ soldats dans le bistro quand la bombe a explosé.

2. -- Où as-tu trouvé _____ robe si élégante?

   -- Chez Pantin. Elle est bien jolie, n'est-ce pas?

3. -- Jean ne va pas venir, j'en suis sûr.

   -- Comment peux-tu dire _____? On peut toujours compter sur lui.

4. -- Comment _____ va?

5. -- Tout le monde est en classe à cette heure-ci, n'est-ce pas?

   -- En principe, oui, mais j'ai vu _____ étudiants devant la fac quand je suis

   entré.

6. -- Tu peux faire _____?

   -- Oui, _____ est très facile à faire.

7. Ils connaissent bien _____ hôtel. Ils y descendent _____ fois

   qu'ils viennent à Paris.

8. _____ prof ne me plaît pas du tout.

F. *Cassette.* Mixed verb drill.

G. *Cassette.* This is both a familiar word and sound discrimination exercise and an opportunity for you to focus on verb forms. Rewrite the word that you hear--one of the forms of a given verb in each case. Note that the various forms will often sound the same: you have to recognize the proper form by the rest of the context.

1. / parlé - parler - parlait /   _____

2. / avez - avaient - aurez /   _____

3. / conduirai - conduiriez - conduire /   _____

4. / discuter - discuté - discutait /   _____

5. / devrais - devais - devras /   _____

6. / saurai - serez - serai / *   _____

   *Note: Two different verbs listed

7. / voyagerez - voyagerais - voyagerai /   _____

H. *Written.* Complete each of the sentences using the appropriate verb, in its proper form, from the list below. NB: Add *à* or *de* before an infinitive, if required.

/ __ faire   __ nettoyer   __ aller   __ voir   __ boire /

1. Nous leur avons suggéré _____ en vacances à Paris.
2. Si nous allions au cinéma ce soir, nous _____ un film comique.
3. Je veux que vous _____ vos devoirs.
4. Elle a aidé son ami _____ sa chambre.

I. *Cassette.* State whether or not the response in each mini-dialogue is logical and appropriate. Write *oui* if it is, *non* if it is not.

1. _____   2. _____   3. _____

J. *Cassette. Dictée.* (Usual format)

1. _____, _____,
2. _____
3. _____.
4. _____
5. _____
6. _____
7. _____
8. _____
9. _____,
10. _____
11. _____.

K. *Written. Composition.* Your vocabulary and your ability to express yourself in French have grown more than you realize. Prove to us that we're right in saying that by going back to the *lecture* in *Intégration: 4-6* and rereading (easily and quickly now) the four poems by Jacques Prévert. Then select one of them as the point of departure for a composition: your reaction to the poem. Don't try to write a *critique* of the poem; just tell us what it makes you think of. Use 8 1/2 X 11 lined paper and double-space, writing on one side only: that should be long enough unless your handwriting is very large.

Chapitre Vingt-Deux

A. *Cassette.* Listen to the dialogue that is on the cassette. As in the last chapter, we do not provide any written text: you must work only with the recorded version.

B. *Written.* Review of object pronouns and adverbial pronouns. Fill in the blanks with the appropriate object form. This should be easy, but be sure to complete this exercise before going on to the next one and to the oral exercise in *D.*

1.   As-tu vendu ta voiture?

         -- Oui, je _____ ai vendue à Philippe.

2. a. Vos parents sont en France maintenant?

         -- Oui, ils _____ vont chaque année.

   b. Ah bon! Alors, vous êtes seul à la maison jusqu'au mois de septembre?

         -- Non, ils _____ reviennent le 15 août.

3.   Quand est-ce que tu vas écrire une lettre à Jean-Paul?

         -- Je ne sais pas. Je _____ ai écrit une carte postale hier.

         -- Ça suffit, j'espère.

4.   C'est ton père qui t'a donné ce parfum?

         -- Oui, il _____ offre souvent du parfum. Il sait que j'adore ça.

5.   Comment va ta femme?

       --Bien, mais elle est fatiguée. Sa sœur est venue _____ rendre

visite hier soir et elles _____ sont parlé jusqu'à trois heures du matin!

6.   Où vas-tu passer tes vacances?

       --Au Caire. Je n' _____ suis jamais allée, et des amis égyptiens _____ ont

invitée.

C. *Cassette.*   Preparation for an exam on reading aloud. This is a sample of one part of an individual oral exam that we give at the end of the second semester using this text. Whether your instructor gives the same kind of exam or not, you will find it useful to practice your pronunciation and intonation in this exercise. The most effective procedure to follow is first to listen to the recording three or four times while looking at the text below. Then read aloud, while listening (as though you were dubbing a film with your voice). Mimic the voices on the tape as closely as you can, paying close attention to intonation, speed, and pauses as well as to the pronunciation of specific sounds.

1.   pont / route / le fils / sœur / vin / vu / c'est moi
2.   bon / se raser / machine / fleur / vingt / lu / la loi
3.   mon / le riz / vite / l'heure / main / du / je bois
4.   Le dictionnaire est sur l'étagère.
5.   Cette question est trop difficile, monsieur.
6.   La nation est divisée en trois régions.
7.   Prend-il toujours ses repas au restaurant?
8.   Allez-vous souvent à ce grand hôtel?
9.   Est-ce qu'elle comprend facilement vos questions?
10.   Pourquoi est-ce que tu fermes les yeux quand tu conduis?
11.   Combien de fois avez-vous vu ce vieux film?
12.   Comment s'appelle la jeune fille qui veut nous accompagner au bal?
13.   N'y touchez pas!
14.   Ne me regardez pas comme ça!
15.   Ne lui donnez jamais rien!

D. *Written.* Answer the following questions, replacing all noun phrases with pronouns or adverbial pronouns, as appropriate. Your answers should be natural and--because of the content of the questions--they will require the use of direct or indirect object pronouns, or adverbial pronouns, or disjunctive pronouns (as well as subject pronouns, of course). Supply additional information as you find appropriate and/or use what we give you in parentheses.

1. Avez-vous déjà visité l'Italie?

    _____

2. Pendant combien de temps es-tu resté chez Nicole?

    _____

3. Où est-ce qu'on produit beaucoup de café?   (Côte d'Ivoire)

    _____

4. Quand es-tu allée au Japon avec ton mari?   (en 1978)

    _____

5. Qu'est-ce que tu vas offrir à Robert comme cadeau de Noël?

    _____

6. La caissière: -À qui avez-vous payé cette chemise, monsieur?   (la vendeuse)

    Le monsieur: _____

7. Vous n'avez pas encore fait vos devoirs, n'est-ce pas? (ce matin)

    _____

8. Quelle langue européenne est-ce qu'on parle en Algérie?

    _____

9. Quand est-ce que tu penses à ces événements?

    _____

E. *Cassette.* Answer the following questions, replacing the direct or indirect objects by pronouns and using the partial answer given to you by the second voice.

Model: You hear: Qu'est-ce que vous avez envoyé à votre frère?
Then you hear, quickly: une photo
You say: **Je lui ai envoyé une photo.**

F. *Written.* Complete the following conditional sentences.

1. J'aurais réussi dans ce cours si _____

   _____

2. Si l'entrée était gratuite, nous _____

   _____

3. Si Jules César n'avait pas conquis la Gaule, _____

   _____

4. Tu aurais pu m'entendre si _____

   _____

5. Si j'avais su qu'elle allait réagir ainsi, _____

   _____

G. *Written.* Complete the blanks with *ce (c')*, *il (elle, ils, elles)*, or *à* or *de*.

1. Comment? Tu ne peux pas le faire? Regarde. Tu vois? _____ est facile.

2. Il est souvent plus difficile _____ convaincre ses amis que de vaincre ses ennemis.

3. _____ est gentille, ta sœur?

4. Tiens. Il y a du poisson. Sers-toi. _____ est bon _____ manger.

5. _____ est vous qui avez réparé ce vélo?

6. _____ est bon _____ changer vos dollars en francs français avant de partir.

7. Où est Alphonse? Je ne sais pas. _____ n'est pas ici.

8. -- Marie vient de téléphoner. Elle ne peut pas nous accompagner.

   -- _____ est dommage. On m'a dit que _____ est un très bon film. Elle l'aurait apprécié.

Nom _____ **Cours** _____ **Section** _____

H. *Written.* Make up a verb pool exercise: Write five sentences, each one using an irregular verb (just leaf through the verb tables, or go back to verb presentations in earlier chapters). At least one sentence must require the present tense, one the *futur proche,* one the *passé composé.* Draw a blank line in each sentence for the verb form that is to be entered. Give infinitives directly below.

/ __   __   __   __

     __   __   /

1. _____

2. _____

3. _____

4. _____

5. _____

I. *Cassette.* State whether or not the response is logical and appropriate.

1. _____   2. _____   3. _____   4. _____

I. *Cassette. Dictée.*

1. _____.
2. _____.
3. _____.
4. _____.
5. _____.
6. _____,
7. _____.
8. _____.
9. _____.
10. _____.

K. *Written.* A composition choice. Either (1) tell us what you think Toto will do now (where he will go; what adventures he will have; with whom?), or (2) continue the story of Philippe (Who is the young lady he is walking off with? Are they going to be married, or just remain good friends? What has he decided to do in life? Will he forget Toto?). Write your answer on one side of an 8 1/2 X 11 piece of lined paper, double-spaced, one-inch margins left and right.